ACCESSING EXCELLENCE AT C.W. POST

Editors

Susan Rock
Chad Coates
Stephen Greco

Long Island University/C.W. Post Campus

KENDALL/HUNT PUBLISHING COMPANY
4050 Westmark Drive   Dubuque, Iowa 52002

NOTE: No University employees were compensated for their time or contributions in the publication of this textbook.

Chapters 1–9 and cover image provided by Long Island University/C.W. Post Campus
Chapter 10 photos from Photos.com

CONTENTS

INTRODUCTION

Welcome to your freshman year at C.W. Post. As you will discover, there are many differences between high school and college. One of those differences is that you are choosing to be a college student. By making that choice, you have begun to take charge of your life and your future. Congratulations!

College 101 is a one credit pass/fail course designed to assist you in transitioning from high school to college. College is a time of challenge and change. How you choose to meet the challenges and changes you face will determine your ultimate success in College 101. You will learn a variety of ways to meet the challenges of college life, work to set some personal goals, and become familiar with the C.W. Post campus and services.

Your success also depends on the moral and ethical decisions you will make, your commitment to accomplishing the goals you will set, your willingness to take advantage of new experiences and opportunities, and your continued motivation. This course will assist you to clarify your values. You will learn time management skills, good study habits, and financial management. In addition, you will explore the relationship between personal life, academic work, and involvement in campus life.

The choice to pursue a college education is the first of many choices you will make in the course of your life. We, the editors of your textbook, hope the skills and strategies you will learn in this course will help you make positive choices that will lead to your success both in college and in life.

Susan Rock
Director, The Learning Support Center

Chad Coates
Assistant Director, The Learning Support Center

Stephen Greco
Senior Peer Mentor

CHAPTER 1 WHY COLLEGE?

Campus Culture:
What Is Expected of College Students Today?

Instructor Expectations

Your individual instructor's expectations are contained in his/her course syllabus. You should get one for every course. The syllabus is your contract with that instructor. It should tell you the course objectives, the name(s) of the textbook(s), grading policies, special requirements, and give you a schedule of assignments. Most instructors distribute the syllabus during the first class period. That's why it's so important to be there for the first class. Some of the information given at that time will not be repeated later, but you will be held accountable for knowing it. Instructors expect you to keep track of your syllabus and follow the schedule, even it they never mention it again. The minimum expectations of most instructors are that you attend class on a regular basis, participate in class discussions and activities, complete your assignments on time, and take tests and examinations when they are given.

In college classes you will be held to much higher standards than you were in high school. You will be expected to study more and devote more time to doing homework. The typical rule is that you should spend at least two hours studying outside of class for every hour you spend in class. Often you are required to do more extensive readings of textbooks and/or supplemental readings. In most courses a portion of your grade is based on writing assignments. These can range from journals or short papers to longer essays or even extensive term papers involving research. Many instructors ask that your work be typewritten, and always expect that it will be clean, neat, and well organized. Non-compliance could lower your grade. Late work may not be accepted at all. In college you are responsible for your learning. No one will remind you to complete your assignments or do your homework. If you miss too many classes you may be dropped for non-attendance.

■ Student Expectations

When you thought about what you expected college to be like, did you consider the ways in which it is different from high school? Depending on your high school experience, college may be similar or it may be very different. Take a moment and brainstorm (generate ideas) a list of all the ways college may be different for you. We started with some examples.

- ■ Tuition is charged
- ■ You buy your own books
- ■ You choose your school
- ■ Each program has its own requirements

_____

_____

_____

_____

■ Student Concerns about Starting College

Starting college can cause a certain amount of fear or apprehension. If you were not a strong student in high school you may be nervous about your study skills and your ability to do college level work. Other people worry about relationships and personal problems that will arise. Going to school requires a definite time commitment for attending classes and studying. Significant others may not understand that you are going to be busier than you were before. Child care arrangements and employment schedules may be more complicated than ever. There will be financial considerations, especially if you are not working.

Student Rights

As college students and adults you have certain rights that go beyond those of high school students. In high school many of the decisions were made for you. Now that you are taking total responsibility for your education you are also entitled to know your rights.

A. You have the right to be treated with dignity and respect by your fellow students and all college employees.

That means everyone from the president of the college to the campus police; from your instructors to the bookstore clerks and cafeteria workers.

B. You have the right to receive a quality education.

Many colleges are even going so far as to issue educational guarantees. For example, if you get an academic degree (Associate of Arts or Associate of Science) from a community college, it will transfer to the public universities in your state. If you get a vocational degree (Associate in Applied Science) you should have the skills to get a job in your field.

C. You have the right to pursue your education in an environment that is safe and conducive to learning.

Usually the campus has a security or police department to insure that students, their cars, and their belongings are safe. While they cannot promise that nothing will ever get stolen from your car, or that your book bag will remain untouched if you leave it in the cafeteria for two hours, they are routinely patrolling the parking lots and buildings on campus. Many departments have security cameras that allow an officer to monitor all of the parking lots and building entrances at once. Other duties of the campus police include parking, traffic regulations, vehicle stickers, fire safety, escort services, as well as crime prevention. Many security offices also assist students by presenting crime awareness programs, and publishing the campus crime statistics. You have a right to know the amount and nature of crimes that are committed on campus.

An environment that is conducive to learning is one that is free of sexual harassment or any other behavior that is unwelcome, degrading, destructive, and unnecessary. Most schools do have written policies regarding sexual harassment stating what is and is not acceptable behavior, and the disciplinary action for what is not acceptable. Everyone must be made aware of these policies, which are usually in the college catalog and student handbook. Be sure that your behavior is appropriate, and do not allow someone else to violate acceptable standards.

D. You have the right to your own opinion.

Although others in the class or on campus may not share your views, you have all of the constitutional rights to freedom of speech and expression. Remember, though, this does not give you the right to monopolize class time voicing your opinion.

E. You have the right to have your privacy respected.

The Family Educational Rights and Privacy Act (FERPA) is a federal law that gives you the right to know what is contained in your school records. It also protects the privacy of your records. Without your permission the college cannot give out information about your schedule, grades, academic standing, test scores, and such, even to your parents or spouse. That is the reason you must request in writing when you want your transcripts or placement test scores sent to another school. The college is allowed to issue directory information (name, address, etc.), but many schools today will not even release that information, especially over the phone. If you do not wish information about yourself given out, you can request that the college not provide this directory information to anyone.

F. You have the right to appeal instructor-initiated withdrawals.

G. You have the right to seek guidance.

The college offers academic advisors in every major to assist students with educational planning. Advisors can also help locate internships or job opportunities in their field. Even if you are a part-time student and were not assigned an advisor, you can request one. The counselors in the counseling office are another source of advice on educational and career planning. They can also help with limited personal issues.

H. You have the right to express concern or dissatisfaction with any situation that impedes your pursuit of education.

Find out what the grievance procedures are on your campus. Follow through until your problem is resolved. Remember, there are levels of authority in any institution. Usually the best results are obtained when you follow the chain of command.

I. You have the right to withdraw from any course until the withdrawal deadline date.

J. You have the right to a final course review if you feel the instructor's final grade for the course has not been fair.

Contact the instructor first to see if you can solve the problem at that level. If not, go to the department chairperson. Follow the procedure outlined in your catalog or handbook.

■ Student Responsibilities

One reason some students do not do well in college is they do not fully understand their responsibilities. Although many students enjoy the increased freedoms of being in college, they seem to forget that with increased freedom comes responsibilities.

In college there is definitely a shift or transferring of responsibility to the student as an adult in charge of his/her own life.

A. It is your responsibility to recognize and respect the rights of other students.

Talk softly in study areas or near classes that are in session. Be quiet in the library, and return your books when they are due. Don't damage books that others will need to use. If you are able bodied be sure to give priority use of the designated elevators and rest rooms to persons with disabilities. They don't have the option of using the stairs or other facilities.

B. It is your responsibility to treat others with dignity and respect.

In class discussions listen to what others have to say and don't make fun of someone else's remarks. Respect your instructors and fellow students. Don't disrupt the class by chatting with the person next to you during the lecture. It is also disruptive to the instructor and the rest of the class when students "pack-up" 10 to 15 minutes before the end of the period. It is obvious they think there won't be anything of importance said. Some even put their coats on and sit on the edge of their chairs, ready to bolt out of the room the second class is dismissed. This behavior is rude, but it is also self-defeating because the end of the period is when the instructor gives instructions for an assignment, reviews hints for the test, or provides other helpful information.

C. You are responsible for your behavior on campus.

Be responsible to clean up your own mess, don't litter, smoke only in the designated areas, don't steal from others, obey the laws for driving and parking, act in a mature, adult manner in classrooms, student lounge areas, and hallways.

D. It is your responsibility to ask when you do not understand something or when you need help.

For example, if you need special services or tutoring, it is up to you to contact the appropriate department or program. You should make appointments to see your advisor for registration or academic planning. Don't wait for someone else to call you first. You may never get what you need.

E. It is your responsibility to attend and participate in class.

The attendance policy will vary with each course and each instructor. Many college students believe they can make their own decisions about whether or not to attend class. This is always a bad idea. Some instructors may allow you to miss class occasionally for good reason, but think about all that you are going to miss by not being there. A large percentage of the material you will be required to know from the class comes from the lecture. If you know in advance that you cannot attend or if you are ill and must miss a class, notify the instructor. Do whatever you can to make up the work. Submit any assignments due that day.

F. If the instructor is late for class it is your responsibility to wait at least 10 to 15 minutes before you leave.

Everyone has emergencies and anyone can be tied up in traffic, so it is only common courtesy to wait. Should the instructor come after you have left, you will be responsible for the missed material.

G. It is your responsibility to do your homework assignments and turn them in on time.

You are also responsible to be aware of what the assignments are, in other words, to read the syllabus.

H. It is your responsibility to read class materials.

Students must read materials in order to be prepared to ask and answer questions, participate in discussions, and to offer comments in class.

I. It is your responsibility to be an active learner.

This is your education. You have to take the initiative to learn, even if the instructor is boring, unfair, not cool, doesn't like you, etc. Failing a course because you don't like the instructor hurts only yourself. Regardless of who the teacher is, it is your responsibility to do the assignments and go to class prepared to learn.

J. It is your responsibility to be aware of college policies and procedures and the chain of command.

When you have a problem to resolve, it is most effective to follow through with the person who has the authority to implement the solution.

K. Some policies that are a must to know:

1. Course prerequisites. These are found in your college catalog.

2. Payment policies and deadline dates. This information is usually listed on the registration information, or on your bill and on your schedule.

3. Course withdrawal procedures and deadline dates. These are described in the catalog and handbook.

4. Instructor requirements, including attendance policies. You will find this in the course syllabus.

5. Academic, Financial, and Veterans' Standards of Progress. See the college catalog and/or get this info from the financial aid and veterans offices.

6. Major/graduation requirements. These are in the college catalog.

7. Appeals processes. Once again, the catalog is the place to look for this.

L. You are responsible for knowing the information in the Student Code of Conduct and for managing your behavior accordingly.

M. It is your responsibility as a student to try to understand another person's perspectives.

Just as you have the right to speak your mind, you have the responsibility to allow others to do the same. Everyone will not think the same way on any given issue. One of the purposes of education is to get you to think with an open mind, to evaluate what you see and hear, and to develop and use logic and reasoning skills.

N. It is your responsibility to provide thoughtful feedback to instructors on evaluations.

Fill out the course evaluation as honestly and thoroughly as you can whenever you are asked to do so. Add written comments. Even your instructors will value your opinion if you are constructive in your critique. They may improve their teaching techniques to benefit future students.

O. It is your responsibility NOT to develop bad habits.

Students should not talk during class, chew gum, eat, or drink noisily, be late for class, create a disturbance, sleep during class, cut classes, be unprepared, not pay attention, or be apathetic.

P. It is your responsibility as well as your right to participate in student activities.

If you want to make things better, get involved. If you don't like the speakers or entertainment offered on campus, volunteer to be on next year's selection committee. Joining student government, the newspaper staff, or any variety of campus clubs will give you valuable leadership experience as well as an opportunity to make the college better for other students like yourself.

Q. You are responsible for checking your progress with your instructors.

You may be given a midterm report, but it is usually not required by the college. It is up to the students to keep track of grades received on assignments, tests, and quizzes. For an accurate report, make an appointment to meet with the teacher in his/her office to see how you are doing.

R. It is your responsibility to evaluate your time commitments and manage your schedule accordingly.

Everyone has things they must do. It is up to you, however, not to schedule doctor, dentist, or other appointments that will conflict with your class time. You will also need to plan for homework and study time in addition to the hours you spend in class. The more roles you have, the more difficult this will be. But, it is not the instructor's fault if you wait to do an assignment until the night before it is due, have an emergency arise and can't get the assignment done on time.

S. It is your responsibility to accept the consequences if you do not do what you should.

■ Instructor Rights

Since there are two parties in the teacher/learner relationship, we thought it would be appropriate to acquaint you with the rights and responsibilities of your instructors. The status given to faculty may vary from campus to campus, and full time teachers may have more influence than part timers, but overall they have some basic assumptions about what should happen. These are things that you should understand as well.

A. Instructors have the right to expect students to arrive on time.

It is distracting and annoying to have your train of thought interrupted every time someone else enters the room. Some teachers will close and lock the door to prevent people from entering late. Others may not be quite that strict, but will appreciate a latecomer slipping in as quietly as possible.

B. Instructors have the right to expect students to behave as adults.

Students should pay attention in class, listen and take notes, not disturb the class by talking with friends, getting up, walking around, or leaving early. If you must leave early it is best to mention this to the instructor before class. If you have a disability that necessitates you moving around, let your instructor know in advance. It is perfectly acceptable for you to accommodate your needs, but this should not come as a total surprise to the instructor.

C. Instructors have the right to expect respect from students.

It should never be necessary to shout, use obscenities, or in any other way show disrespect to a teacher. If there is a severe problem that cannot be resolved with the instructor, talk to the department chairperson or the academic dean of the college.

D. Instructors have the right to be notified if students have a problem or concern about their courses.

Always use your instructor as the first resort to seek a solution for any class problem.

E. Instructors have the right to expect students to read the syllabus, to be prepared for class, and to be prepared for tests.

(Bring your own pencils, etc.)

F. Instructors have the right to expect students to seek help during posted office hours, to request make-up materials, or to check on work missed during an absence.

It is really unfair of students to expect the teacher to be a walking file cabinet, carrying all of the handouts from the last three sessions, just in case someone didn't get them or lost their copies. Many teachers have their classes scheduled back to back and in different rooms, which really makes it inconvenient to stay after class to talk to a student who missed a previous session.

G. Instructors have the right not to be expected to calculate grades in their heads or on the spot just because the student caught them in the cafeteria or parking lot.

Even if the teacher has his/her grade book at hand, don't expect to look over his/her shoulder at your grades; that's a breech of confidentiality if other students' grades are on the same page.

H. Instructors have the right to withdraw students from their class for the following reasons:

1. lack of attendance

2. plagiarism

3. lack of satisfactory progress

4. misconduct

I. Instructors have the right of academic freedom.

As degreed professionals they are granted the right to express themselves freely (within the college's code of conduct), to conduct their classes as they see fit, to assign homework, to use outside sources of information as provided by the copyright laws, and determine their own system for grading.

■ Instructor Responsibilities

Your instructors have certain responsibilities to you as students and to the college. Because they seem somewhat self-explanatory, we will not go into great detail about each. Here is a list of several that we thought were important.

It is your instructor's responsibility:

A. To arrive and start class on time.

B. To inform the students in advance if he/she knows class will be cancelled.

C. To cover the material in the syllabus.

D. To treat students and their opinions with respect.

E. To inform students of their progress without violating confidentiality.

F. To provide a learning environment.

G. To present effective lectures that stick to the subject without rambling.

H. To be prepared and organized.

I. To be considerate of the able bodied and the disabled student, i.e., not speaking too fast or in a monotone, leaving transparencies or visual aids on the screen long enough to take notes, and willingly providing reasonable accommodations for students with disabilities.

J. To explain concepts, and to repeat or reteach if necessary.

K. To be in their office during posted office hours and to keep scheduled appointments.

L. Not to:

1. keep class beyond the end of the period

2. show partiality or favoritism

3. embarrass students

4. behave as if their class is the only class the student is taking

5. behave as if their opinion is the only opinion

■ Becoming a Student

By this time you may already be enrolled in your first semester of college. You may have been through the admission and registration processes. In that case you have already selected your first classes and been to the bookstore to buy your first textbooks, including this one. For those of you who may be still in high school, let's talk for a moment about the admissions process.

Orientation

Most colleges provide some type of orientation program for their new students. It may be required or it may be voluntary. Participating in whatever kind of orientation your school has is always a good idea. This is your opportunity to learn about the environment where you will be spending the next years. Every attempt will be made to inform you of the services and facilities that your college offers, but if there is some service not mentioned, ask questions. It is still your responsibility to seek out help.

Registration

The registration process varies from college to college. Most offer an open registration period that lasts until the semester begins. Some schools may even allow you to register the opening week of classes. The earlier you get your schedule set, however, the better. Once a class has the maximum number of students enrolled, it will be closed. Sections with the best times and the best teachers always fill up first. I've seen popular classes become full during the first hour of registration! So, get started as soon as possible. If you ended up with a lot of leftovers this semester, that should convince you to register early next semester.

Academic Advisors

Full-time students are usually assigned an academic advisor. Academic advisors may be full- or part-time faculty, administrators, or other staff that provide assistance with deciding on a major, selecting courses, teaching study skills, or a number of other services for students. Find out what your school's policy is regarding academic advising. Is there an Academic Advising Center? Have you been assigned to an academic advisor? Be sure to make good use of any service that is offered in this area. Find out who your advisor is and schedule an appointment. When you meet with him/her, bring along the college catalog, your placement test results, the schedule of classes for the semester, an advisor summary listing all previous courses taken at your institution, and/or transcripts from other colleges and universities. By having everything you need, you will make the best use of your time with your advisor.

Your advisor can also help you rearrange your schedule, if that becomes necessary. If you find out within the first week of classes that your work/practice schedule has changed, or that a particular course or instructor isn't what you thought and you know you'll never survive an entire semester, try to rearrange your schedule immediately. There is probably a refund period during which you can get your money back if you withdraw from a class. Make sure you follow the college's add/drop procedure for making those changes. There may be penalties for procrastination or not following the proper procedure. Failure to follow all the steps may result in your not being withdrawn during the refund period. Remember, too, that there is a final withdrawal date after which you cannot drop a class for any reason. If you don't withdraw by that date, the instructor must give you a grade for the course.

Core Curriculum

Most colleges have some kind of core curriculum. This means that all students are required to take the same group of courses. The purpose of these courses is to provide you with a well rounded education, not just to prepare you for an occupation.

Grades/Grade Point Average

Grades are used to evaluate your success in school at the end of each semester. Students who intend to transfer or graduate need to be concerned about their Grade Point Average (GPA). Your grade point average is determined by the number of credits you attempt during a term. Each grade is assigned a value and is worth a certain number of quality points. Most colleges use a 4.0 grading system, although some colleges have a 5.0 grading system.

A = 4 points	A = 5 points
B = 3 points	B = 4 points
C = 2 points	C = 3 points
D = 1 point	D = 2 points
E/F = 0 points	E = 1 point
	F = 0 points

To figure your Grade Point Average, multiply the number of quality points for the grade you received by the number of credits for the course. Total the quality points for all the courses and total the number of hours you attempted in the semester. Then divide the total quality points by the total number of attempted hours. An Incomplete grade does not receive any points until the course is finished. If a course offers a grade of Pass/Fail or Satisfactory/Unsatisfactory the credits will count for graduation, but the grade for the course does not compute into your GPA.

Tuition and Fees

You will be charged tuition for every credit hour in which you enroll. Variable course fees for such things as photocopies, computer time, and lab equipment are charged in addition to tuition. The course fee is usually listed on the schedule. The college may add other fees such as a registration or testing fee, and you will also be charged a student activity fee. This money helps pay for such things as student clubs, entertainment, special speakers, the school newspaper, literary magazine, or other publications that are distributed free to students.

Financial Aid

If you need assistance with your tuition, fees, books, and supplies, visit the Financial Aid Office on your campus to see what might be available to you. This office coordinates all sources of financial aid including scholarships, grants, loans, work-study programs, and deferred payment plans. Ask any financial aid officer for the appropriate forms for federal and state financial aid programs in order to see if you qualify.

Campus Resources

The Campus

Your college has many resources to help you with a wide variety of needs. The campus itself is a resource. The buildings and grounds are maintained so that you will have an accessible place to study and attend classes. There are parking lots for staff, students, and visitors. There may be a bus stop or stops for other forms of public transportation. Every campus will have a bookstore where you can buy your textbooks, school supplies, clothes with the college logo, greeting cards, snacks, and other items. Campus maps help newcomers find their way around. There will be a campus police or security station. There may be other conveniences such as a photocopy center or ATM machine.

Food service on campus may range from vending machines to a full service cafeteria. Depending on the campus, the cafeteria may be open for breakfast, lunch, and dinner on a daily basis. Another important resource for students is the information center which is usually centrally located to help with the following services: general information, payment for everything from tuition to traffic tickets, switchboard, and student computer stations that let you personally access your schedule, records, etc.

Academic Support Services

Learning Resource Center/Library

It always amazes me when students who have been on campus for more than a semester don't know where to find the Learning Resource Center (LRC). Even if you don't have a research paper to write, the college library offers the perfect place to study in peace and quiet. Current popular books, magazines, and newspapers are available to read for pleasure in addition to the scholarly publications needed for research. The LRC offers a variety of other services such as a place to view video tapes, use computers or word processors, duplicate materials, and may be the center for telecourses.

Academic Skills Center

The academic skills center is a good place to learn. It offers assistance with study skills, time management, and note taking. It also provides free or inexpensive tutoring services for students. The academic skills center may be the place to make up missed exams, to take placement tests, or to use when you need extended time on a test. Again you will need to check your individual college's policies regarding the skills center.

Tutoring

Tutoring services are available in many schools at no extra cost or low cost to students. Find out where tutoring is available at your school. Academic skills centers and specialized programs offer these support services. A tutor may be another student, a faculty member, or a professional staff person whose primary responsibility is assisting students with their academic work. In any event that person is skilled in his/her subject area and trained to work with small groups or with a student on an individual basis. Tutoring may be available to you as a walk-in or by appointment only.

If you have made an appointment with a tutor be sure that you keep the appointment and come prepared. Do not expect the tutor to do your work for you or to make up for missed classes. Read your textbook, work your assignments, and write down any problems or unanswered questions you might have. Bring all your work to the tutoring session. If you cannot keep your appointment be sure to call the tutoring office to cancel. There may be other students waiting to use that valuable time.

Mentors

Mentors are usually volunteers who assist students in adjusting to college. They may be faculty, staff persons, or members of the community to whom you can turn when the going gets rough. These people are dedicated individuals who give of their time freely and have made a difference in the lives of many students.

Academic Computing Labs

There are places on campus where you can use computers to do your assignments. They are usually staffed with a lab assistant to help you if you need it. Academic computing labs are not where you learn how to use a computer; that's why computer science courses are offered.

Specialized Labs

Often the college will have specialized labs for practicing what you are learning in foreign language classes. Computer assistance or audio tapes may be available to increase your vocabulary, verb conjugation, pronunciation, and conversation fluency.

There may be a writing lab for students who need to develop their writing skills. This can be an excellent way to learn as some of these labs offer extraordinary supplemental instruction. If you are taking a writing course this lab should be a must on your list of sites to visit.

A basic skills lab may offer computer-based learning to enhance your skills in all areas of reading, writing, and math. This lab is a MUST for all developmental education students. Locate and become familiar with the services of any specialized labs on your campus.

Disabled Student Services

If you have a documented physical or learning disability, you are entitled by law to **reasonable** accommodations because of your disability. Most campuses have an office that coordinates these services. They might range from enlarging reading material, providing note takers, arranging for sign language interpreters, furnishing desks in classrooms to accommodate wheelchairs and other physical disabilities, and allowing instructors the facilities to give untimed tests. They may provide equipment such as tape recorders, calculators, magnifiers, automatic page turners, computer voice synthesizers, recorded textbooks, and large print dictionaries. Professional tutors may also be available to help students with learning disabilities. Students with limited English speaking proficiency, students whose academic skill level interferes with success in their classes, and students with health concerns can be eligible to receive services as well.

Your campus may have a variety of special programs to meet the needs of specific target populations. Some may provide counseling and tutorial services beyond those regularly offered on campus. The money to pay for these programs usually comes from federal or state funds, given to the college in the form of a grant. With these extra resources grant programs can enhance your opportunities to achieve your academic goals.

Student Services

Counseling

Most college counseling centers are staffed by professionals who have degrees in counseling or psychology. Many are licensed by the state or by their profession to help students with academic and personal issues. If you need assistance with choosing a major, selecting courses, or just feel the need to talk to someone about where you are going and what you are doing, be sure to stop in your college's counseling center. Services are usually free. Your visits and anything you discuss with the counselor will always be kept confidential.

Career Center

The career center may or may not be part of the counseling center on your campus. This is where you can find material for career exploration. Interest inventories and other assessment instruments are usually available to students for the purpose of discovering their career options. Computerized versions of career guidance information systems may also be available in your center.

Placement Center

This office on campus helps students and alumni to get jobs in their career field. The center may bring employers on campus for job fairs or recruiting purposes. Some publish a job bulletin that lists full- and part-time employment opportunities. Often this office handles student worker applications, provides resume writing workshops, helps you to acquire interviewing skills, and assists you in your job search.

Intercultural/Minority Affairs

Intercultural and minority affairs generally supports the recruitment, retention, and graduation of students from groups that are not well represented on college campuses. They may provide services to any protected class such as women, African Americans, Native Americans, Latinos/Latinas, etc.

Health and Wellness

Many people today are concerned with health and well being. The college is a great place to learn better, healthier habits for eating, exercising, and prevention of diseases. Check out the workshops and seminars offered through the health services department or program. If you have a problem with smoking, drug and/or alcohol abuse there are support services available to help you.

Graduation/Records Office

The records office (sometimes called the registrar's office) is where you will find all your student records. Your instructors will be sending your grades to the registrar and it will be this office from which you will receive your report card. If there is any doubt in your mind about the final grade you receive for a class, contact your instructor or the registrar. When transferring to another school or finding employment you will be asked for a transcript of your records.

Student Activities

Athletics and clubs on campus offer students many extracurricular activities. Find one that suits your major, interests, or hobbies.

Student Organizations

You might investigate a number of groups on campus for the sole purpose of extracurricular activities, personal development, making new friends, or just having fun. The athletic department, the health and wellness center, service clubs, awareness groups, religious organizations, music and theater groups, diversity clubs, and honor societies can all add a little spice to your life.

If you are interested in politics, student government may be the avenue for you. It is an excellent training ground for teamwork and leadership and will look terrific on any resume. If your major is media or communications, you may be interested in the student bulletins, newspaper, yearbook, photography/video clubs, or campus radio and TV stations. A number of honor societies invite students with high GPAs and/or specific majors to become members.

Campus Facilities

The college campus has a wealth of facilities that are open to students and residents of the campus. The health and fitness center, gym, swimming pool, athletic fields, tennis courts, and/or bowling alleys on many campuses contribute to the physical well being of the community. The performing arts center, art gallery, planetarium, greenhouse, and/or arcades provide additional recreational opportunities. For many adult students who are parents of young children, the child care center or preschool on campus makes it possible to attend classes and activities with peace of mind. They don't have to worry about finding a reliable babysitter, it is convenient, and they are close at hand should an emergency arise.

Community Outreach Programs

Colleges seek to serve the people living in their community. They offer general interest courses to develop a hobby, to learn a new skill for fun, or for social interaction. These are non-credit classes provided at a reasonable fee as a service to the public. Continuing education courses let people in various professions upgrade their skills, keep current with new trends, and qualify for recertification.

For those who need help with basic reading, writing, and math skills, the college is the place to go. Adult education departments usually offer courses at no cost to the students, and often even provide the textbooks. Volunteer literacy tutors give one-on-one instruction to adults who wish to learn to read (or to read better). Some colleges have programs that give books to needy families to encourage children and their parents to read. English as a Second Language (ESL) classes help beginners and advanced speakers master the English language. GED test preparation, though, is probably the most popular feature of adult education. Special graduation ceremonies are often held to honor those who have attained their high school equivalency diploma.

Most colleges reach out to business and industry. They provide assessment and training for employees, help with small business development, and may have special programs for dislocated workers (people out of work because of lay offs, plant closings, or downsizing).

Music, art, and theater events are open to the public and provide cultural opportunities for the community. Youth college offers children a chance to be involved with fun and educational classes at their own level, while elder college encourages senior citizens to stay active. Other community outreach programs might include support groups, athletic events, family activities, job fairs, college fairs, and providing facilities for meetings, festivals, or research.

Community Services Available

The community, in turn, provides the college with many services to benefit students. Bus transportation is often available to most campus centers and satellites. Local newspapers, radio and TV stations inform the public of current events on the campus, and the college has an outlet for advertising their activities to the community. Health care services, counseling, community hot lines, programs such as the Private Industry Council, Displaced Homemakers, and Public Aid supplemental projects assist students.

■ Summary

We have explored your expectations for college. We also discussed in detail the rights and responsibilities of you, the student, and the rights and responsibilities of your instructors. The remainder of the chapter acquaints you with the resources on campus and in the community, all of which will enable you to become good college students.

In addition, one of the best campus resources is your faculty. They want you to succeed and get a good education so that you will have a strong foundation for life. That is the reason that they are in the classroom. If you are successful, they are successful. The faculty on your campus, however, expect that you will take responsibility for your education. Make the best use you can of all your campus resources and services. They are there to help you.

CHAPTER 2 WELLNESS
Maintaining a Healthy Lifestyle

Healthy Lifestyles through Wellness

How are you? You probably answered "fine" without really thinking. But, how do you **really** feel . . . about yourself, your life, your lifestyle, your health? Chances are that you may not have considered all of the many facets that constitute your true well-being. Do you eat well? Do you exercise regularly? Do you smoke or drink? Do you have close friends with whom you can share your experiences, both good and traumatic? Are you under extreme stress to get good grades, perform well on the job, or be a good parent? Do you get regular medical checkups and do you practice self-care? Are you aware of safety and environmental factors that contribute to your health? This

From *The Freshman Year: Making the Most of College* by Glenda A. Belote and Larry W. Lunsford. © 1998 by Kendall/Hunt Publishing Company.

chapter will help you develop important strategies that will enable you to live life to the fullest, both physically and emotionally.

Traditionally, health was simply defined as the absence of disease or symptoms. This concept has gradually evolved over the past fifty years so that health is now defined by the World Health Organization as a continuous and harmonious balance of physical, mental, spiritual, intellectual, and social well-being. This continuum of a "balanced," healthy lifestyle has been defined as **wellness.** True wellness involves contracting with yourself to engage in healthy behaviors and attitudes that enhance the quality of your life and personal performance.

To achieve this state of wellness, you must maintain a balance of six continually changing dimensions that affect your overall health. These components of wellness are:

Physical

Physical wellness is the ability to maintain positive lifestyle habits to enable you to perform your daily tasks. Such components of the physical dimension of wellness entail eating healthy foods, maintaining appropriate weight and body fat, performing regular exercise to maintain cardiovascular fitness, and avoiding the abuse of tobacco, alcohol, and other drugs.

Emotional

Emotional wellness is the ability to manage stress and express your emotions appropriately by recognizing and accepting your feelings about the events in your life. Stress is part of everyone's life, but your ability to properly manage life's stressful events can greatly influence your overall health potential.

Spiritual

The belief in an abstract strength that unites all of your internal energies. This strength can include religion and/or nature, but also includes your values, ethics, and morals. Your personal sense of spirituality provides meaning and direction to your life, enabling you to learn, develop, and meet new challenges successfully.

Social

The skill to interact successfully with other people at work, school, and the community. This dimension of wellness encompasses your ability to handle relationships, both intimate and casual.

Intellectual

The ability to learn and use your knowledge effectively to enhance your overall health. Knowledge of self-care techniques, disease risk factors, as well as your family history of disease, are all important components to achieving intellectual wellness.

Environmental

The physical and social setting that influences your lifestyle. This dimension includes your personal safety practices, such as wearing seat belts, to your efforts to help promote a clean environment.

These six dimensions of wellness overlap, and components of one often can directly or indirectly affect factors in another. Some health parameters are under your direct control and some are not. For example, your lifestyle behaviors (diet, exercise, habits) constitute the greatest percentage of influences on the quality of your life.

Relationships involving family, friends, and the community are also important, as are factors pertaining to the quality of health care you receive by physicians and health care facilities. Approximately 85 percent of the factors influencing your health are within your control. The remaining 15 percent are beyond your individual control and consist of heredity predispositions. If your medical history reveals a family tendency toward a specific disease, such as heart disease or cancer, your lifestyle decisions can delay the onset, minimize the disease's effects, or possibly even prevent the disease from occurring. This is why a good knowledge of preventive medicine becomes so important.

■ Health Benefits of Wellness

You can achieve wellness through improving your knowledge about health, eliminating risk factors, practicing good self-care habits and preventive medicine, and maintaining a positive attitude. Some of the benefits of wellness include:

- a decreased risk of developing chronic diseases;
- a decreased risk of accidents;
- a decreased recovery time after injury and illness;
- an improved cardiovascular system function (heart efficiency and blood vessel diameter both increase);
- an increased muscle tone, strength, and flexibility;
- an improved physical appearance—less fat, greater muscle tone;
- an increased ability to manage stress and resist depression;
- proper nutrition for optimal growth, repair, immune function, and development;
- a higher self-esteem;
- an increased energy level, productivity, and creativity; and
- an improved awareness of your personal needs and the ways to achieve them.

■ Wellness as a Challenge

Your belief in your ability to perform healthy behaviors will influence your actual choices, your degree of effort to make the change, your persistence, and your emotional reactions to the new lifestyle. Your ability to turn your health-related goals into reality is dependent on formulating a plan of action. This lifestyle modification has several steps:

Step 1. Evaluate your personal health habits. Make a list of your behaviors that promote health and make another list of your behaviors that are harmful. Once you have compiled both of your lists, note which behaviors present the greatest threat to your overall well-being. These behaviors should be targeted for change first.

Step 2. Set realistic, specific, observable, and measurable goals. Don't expect miracles. Setting goals that are too ambitious leads to failure; the fear of failure may discourage future efforts. View lifestyle change as a lifetime change. Strive for moderation rather than striving for complete behavior reversal or abstinence. Behavior changes that are "slow-but-steady" are the ones most likely to result in permanent success.

Step 3. Formulate a strategy for success. Most people want to make positive changes, but too often find reasons why they cannot make changes. They may not have the time, are too tired, or simply feel embarrassed. What are some of your reasons? These barriers to change must be avoided if you are to achieve your healthy goals.

Step 4. Evaluate your progress. How well are you doing? The only way to consistently stick with your new healthy behavior is to receive feedback by monitoring your progress. This evaluation allows you to modify the program, enabling you to better achieve your goals. Initially, the evaluation periods should be frequent, such as daily or weekly. After periods of consistent success, the time interval between evaluation sessions could be lengthened to, perhaps, monthly.

Success does not have to be all-or-nothing. This manner of thinking can be detrimental to your overall motivation to change. When your goals are not fully realized, simply reshape your goals, set a more realistic time schedule, or formulate different intervention strategies, and **TRY AGAIN**. More importantly, answer these questions:

"What did I learn from this experience?"

"What can I do differently?"

Based on your answers, make a revised contract and begin immediately. Remember that lifestyle change is never easy but its rewards will last a lifetime. The exercise on the next page will assist you in planning for a healthier lifestyle.

You Are What You Eat

Dietary habits play a key role in both how long we live and how well we feel. A healthy diet is one that features a proper variety and balance of foods to supply our body with nutrients, essential dietary factors required for growth, energy, and repair. There are six nutrients: proteins, carbohydrates, fats, vitamins, minerals, and water.

Protein is necessary for growth and repair, forming the basic building blocks of muscles, bones, hair, and blood. Meat, poultry, fish, eggs, milk, cheese, dry beans, and nuts are excellent dietary sources of protein.

Carbohydrates provide the body with glucose, its basic fuel. There are two types of carbohydrates: simple and complex. Simple carbohydrates are sugars, which are responsible for providing short bursts of energy. Examples of dietary sugars include glucose, sucrose (table sugar), fructose (the sugar found in fruits), honey, and syrup. Complex carbohydrates consist of starches and fiber, important ingredients of cereals, breads, rice, pasta, fruits, and vegetables. Soluble fiber, found in oats, beans, apples, and citrus fruit, has been shown to lower blood cholesterol levels and decrease the risk of heart disease.

Fats are high calorie nutrients that come in two primary types: saturated and unsaturated. Saturated fats, found in animal products such red meat, egg yolk, and butter, have been shown to increase the blood cholesterol levels and increase the risk of heart disease. In contrast, monounsaturated and polyunsaturated fats are found primarily in foods of plant origin and have been shown to lower blood cholesterol levels. Polyunsaturated fats are found in safflower and corn oils, whereas canola and olive oil are monounsaturated fats. In contrast to protein and carbohydrates, which contain four calories per gram, fat contributes nine calories per gram when metabolized in the body. For this reason, a simple way to lose weight is to decrease the amount of dietary fat.

Vitamins are organic nutrients which work with the body's enzymes to enable biochemical reactions to take place. Vitamins C and E, as well as beta carotene, serve as antioxidants, substances that protect cells from dangerous free radicals produced by normal metabolic processes. Antioxidants have been shown to reduce the incidence of heart disease and certain types of cancer.

Minerals are inorganic substances found in food that are also essential for proper metabolism. Macrominerals (sodium, potassium, calcium, phosphorus, and magnesium) are required in larger amounts than are the trace minerals (iron, zinc, selenium, iodine, chromium, and fluoride). Calcium is the most abundant mineral in the body, responsible for bone integrity and prevention of osteoporosis, as well as for conduction of nerve impulses and cardiac contraction.

Exercise:

Do aerobic exercises (walking, jogging, swimming, cycling, etc.) for 30 minutes three to four times a week.

Incorporate exercise into your daily activities (e.g., take the stairs).

Always do warm-up and cool-down exercises and stretch before and after your aerobic session to improve flexibility and decrease risk of injury.

Nutrition:

Eat foods high in complex carbohydrates (breads, cereals, fruits, vegetables, pasta) to constitute 48 percent of your total daily calories.

Limit simple sugars (table sugar, soft drinks, candy); consume only with meals.

Limit saturated fat intake (animal fats, whole milk, etc.); consume more fat calories as monounsaturated (canola and olive oil) and polyunsaturated (vegetable oils) fats.

Drink at least eight glasses of water daily.

Stress management:

Improve your time management and organizational skills (set priorities, don't procrastinate, make a daily schedule with flexible time and follow it).

Practice progressive muscle relaxation, meditation, yoga, and deep-breathing exercises.

Self-care:

Don't smoke.

Only drink alcohol responsibly; (e.g. don't drink and drive, no more than two or three drinks in one sitting, etc.).

Perform breast or testicular self-exams monthly.

Have regular medical screenings and physical exams.

Know your blood pressure and cholesterol numbers.

Practice abstinence or safer sex (always use condoms).

Sleep at least seven to eight hours daily and develop a regular sleep-wake cycle.

Read about current health topics and medical discoveries; check the Internet.

Safety:

Always wear a seat belt.

Learn cardiopulmonary resuscitation (CPR).

Check smoke detectors in your home annually.

Figure 1 ■ Wellness Strategies for Top Performance: Academically and Athletically

I, _____, pledge that I will accomplish the goals listed below.

—Personal Goal: Improve my fitness level.

—Motivating Factors: I want to have more energy and feel better.

—Change(s) I Promise to Make to Reach This Goal: Jog for 20–30 minutes at least three times a week.

—Start Date: January 1

—Intervention Strategies:

1. I will walk early in the morning before classes.
2. I will walk after classes on days when it is raining in the morning.

Plan for Making This Change:

First week: walk for 10 minutes three times a week.

Weeks 2 to 4: Increase the amount of walking time by five minutes every week until I walk for 20–30 minutes each session.

Week 5: Evaluate my progress.

Weeks 5 to 9: Gradually increase my speed.

Week 10: Evaluate my progress.

After the first 10 weeks: Continue my morning jogs three times a week.

—Target Date for Reaching Goal: March 15

—Reward for Reaching Goal: Buy a new, expensive pair of jogging shoes.

—If I Need Help: I can call my friend _____ to walk or jog with me.

Signed: _____

Witness: _____

Date: _____

Figure 2 ■ A Sample Contract for Lifestyle Change

Approximately 60 percent of your weight consists of **water**. Water helps to digest foods, maintains proper body temperature, lubricates joints, and eliminates the body's waste products via urine. Water is necessary for survival, as we would die after only a few days without water. In contrast, we could survive for several weeks without food. You should drink at least eight glasses of water a day, not counting alcohol and drinks that contain the diuretic caffeine, such as coffee, tea, and certain soft drinks.

■ How Much Should I Eat?

According to the American Dietetic Association, 12 percent of your daily calories should come from protein; 58 percent from carbohydrates (of which 48 percent should be complex carbohydrates and only 10 percent simple sugars); and a total of 30 percent from fats (10 percent saturated fats, 10 percent monounsaturated fats, and 10 percent polyunsaturated fats). In contrast, the typical American diet consists of too much saturated fats and simple sugars, and lacks sufficient amounts of complex carbohydrates. To best help you determine what your daily nutrient intake is, you need to understand the food pyramid.

■ The Food Guide Pyramid

In 1992, the United States Department of Agriculture published the Food Guide Pyramid, a guideline to simplify the selections of foods that constitute a healthy diet. As shown in Figure 3, the Food Guide Pyramid incorporates five food groups plus fats, oils, and sugars. Foods in one category cannot replace those from another.

The foods at the base of the Food Guide Pyramid form the foundation of a healthy diet and consist of foods high in complex carbohydrates—breads, cereals, rice, and pasta. The foods at the Pyramid's base are high in fiber, iron, protein, and B vitamins, and should be consumed in the largest quantities, namely six to eleven servings daily. The second tier of the Food Guide Pyramid consists of vegetables and fruits—foods that are high in fiber, low in fat, and high in vitamins A and C. Scientific studies have revealed that vegetables and fruits may prevent cancers of the lung, colon, stomach, bladder, and breast. According to the Food Guide Pyramid, three to five servings of vegetables and two to four servings of fruits are recommended daily. Foods in the "Milk, Yogurt, and Cheese" group are high in calcium, protein, and vitamins A and B-12. Two servings per day are recommended. Foods in the "Meat, Poultry, Fish, Dry Beans, Eggs, and Nuts" group are excellent sources of protein, iron, zinc, phosphorus, and B vitamins. These foods are also high in fats and cholesterol; thus, you should choose low-fat varieties. Finally, foods at the apex of the pyramid (the smallest part of the pyramid) should be consumed in very small quantities. Fats, oils, and sweets are high in calories but supply little or no vitamins or minerals. Select foods from this category that are high in monounsaturated fats, such as canola or olive oils.

■ Using Your Resources

Visit the campus health center, a primary care physician, or a registered dietician to receive a personal nutrition consultation. A licensed health professional can help you lose weight or gain weight; prescribe a diet to help control blood pressure, diabetes, or high cholesterol; or provide guidance concerning dietary supplements.

Food Guide Pyramid

A Guide to Daily Food Choices

Figure 3 ■ Food Guide Pyramid

■ Responsible Drinking

According to a number of studies, abuse of alcohol is the number-one problem facing college students today. Although more students are choosing to abstain, approximately 85 percent of college students use alcohol. A small percentage of these students drink irresponsibly, either binge drinking (drinking five or more drinks at one sitting), drinking while under the legal drinking age, or driving under the influence of alcohol. The leading cause of death among college students is alcohol-related automobile accidents. The use and abuse of alcohol is also associated with most cases of campus violence, arrests, vandalism, rape, accidents, homicides, unwanted sex, sexually transmitted diseases and HIV/AIDS, unwanted pregnancies, poor grades, and drop-outs.

Alcohol can also impair your judgment. You may actually have sex with someone whom you would normally not even go out to lunch with! However, the consequences of your decision, such as an unintended pregnancy, a sexually transmitted disease, or an accident resulting in a lifelong disability, may last a lifetime.

GRAINS Make half your grains whole	VEGETABLES Vary your veggies	FRUITS Focus on fruits	MILK Get your calcium-rich foods	MEAT & BEANS Go lean with protein
Eat at least 3 oz. of whole-grain cereals, breads, crackers, rice, or pasta every day 1 oz. is about 1 slice of bread, about 1 cup of breakfast cereal, or ½ cup of cooked rice, cereal, or pasta	Eat more dark-green veggies like broccoli, spinach, and other dark leafy greens Eat more orange vegetables like carrots and sweetpotatoes Eat more dry beans and peas like pinto beans, kidney beans, and lentils	Eat a variety of fruit Choose fresh, frozen, canned, or dried fruit Go easy on fruit juices	Go low-fat or fat-free when you choose milk, yogurt, and other milk products If you don't or can't consume milk, choose lactose-free products or other calcium sources such as fortified foods and beverages	Choose low-fat or lean meats and poultry Bake it, broil it, or grill it Vary your protein routine — choose more fish, beans, peas, nuts, and seeds

For a 2,000-calorie diet, you need the amounts below from each food group. To find the amounts that are right for you, go to MyPyramid.gov.

Eat 6 oz. every day	Eat 2 ½ cups every day	Eat 2 cups every day	Get 3 cups every day; for kids aged 2 to 8, it's 2	Eat 5½ oz. every day

Find your balance between food and physical activity
- Be sure to stay within your daily calorie needs.
- Be physically active for at least 30 minutes most days of the week.
- About 60 minutes a day of physical activity may be needed to prevent weight gain.
- For sustaining weight loss, at least 60 to 90 minutes a day of physical activity may be required.
- Children and teenagers should be physically active for 60 minutes every day, or most days.

Know the limits on fats, sugars, and salt (sodium)
- Make most of your fat sources from fish, nuts, and vegetable oils.
- Limit solid fats like butter, stick margarine, shortening, and lard, as well as foods that contain these.
- Check the Nutrition Facts label to keep saturated fats, *trans* fats, and sodium low.
- Choose food and beverages low in added sugars. Added sugars contribute calories with few, if any, nutrients.

MyPyramid.gov
STEPS TO A HEALTHIER YOU

U.S. Department of Agriculture
Center for Nutrition Policy and Promotion
April 2005
CNPP-15

Figure 3 ■ Food Guide Pyramid (continued)

By definition, any drink containing 0.5 percent or more ethyl alcohol by volume is an alcoholic beverage. However, different drinks contain different amounts of alcohol. For example, one drink is defined as any of the following:

- one 12 oz can of beer (5 percent alcohol);
- one 4 oz glass of wine (12 percent alcohol); or
- one shot (1 oz) of distilled spirits, such as whiskey, vodka, or rum (50 percent alcohol). The alcohol content is expressed as **proof**, a number that is twice the percentage of alcohol: 80-proof gin is 40 percent alcohol, etc.

To determine the amount that you can safely drink, you need to determine the blood-alcohol concentration (BAC), the percentage of alcohol in the blood. The BAC is usually measured from your breath. Most people reach a BAC of 0.05 percent after consuming one or two drinks; at this level, they do not feel intoxicated. If they continue to drink past this BAC level, they start to feel worse, with decreased reaction times, slurred speech, and loss of balance and emotional control. The legal BAC in most states is 0.08 percent. Persons driving a motor vehicle with a BAC of 0.08 percent or greater are cited for driving under the influence and are subject to severe legal penalties and fines. At a BAC of 0.2 percent, a person is likely to pass out and at a BAC of 0.3 percent, a person could lapse into a coma. Death is likely with a BAC of 0.4 percent or higher.

These factors will influence your BAC and response to alcohol:

- **How much and how quickly you drink.** If you chug drink after drink, your liver, which can only metabolize 0.5 oz of alcohol per hour, will not be able to keep up, resulting in a rapidly rising BAC.
- **The type of drink.** The stronger the drink, the faster the rise in BAC, and the consequent symptoms. If the drink contains water, juice, or milk, the rate of absorption will be decreased, slowing the rate of BAC rise. However, if you mix an alcoholic drink with carbon dioxide (e.g., champagne or a cola), the rate of alcohol absorption will increase.
- **The temperature of the alcoholic drink.** Warm drinks result in a faster rate of absorption.
- **Food.** Food slows the rate of absorption by interfering with the intestine's absorptive membrane surface. Certain high-fat foods can also prolong the time it takes for the stomach to empty its contents, resulting in delayed absorption times.
- **Your size.** Large people who have excessive fat or muscle tend to have a larger water volume, which dilutes the alcohol consumed. Therefore, large people can drink more alcohol and will get drunk more slowly than small or thin people.
- **Your gender.** Women tend to get drunk more quickly than men. Women possess smaller quantities of a stomach enzyme that metabolizes alcohol. The hormone estrogen also plays a role, as women are more sensitive to the effects of alcohol just prior to menstruation and when they are taking birth control pills that contain estrogen. One drink consumed by a woman will produce roughly the same physiologic consequences as two drinks consumed by a man.
- **Your age.** The older you are, the higher the BAC level will be after consuming equivalent drinks.
- **Your ethnicity.** Certain ethnic groups, such as Asians and Native Americans, are unable to metabolize alcohol as quickly as others including Caucasians and African Americans.
- **Other drugs.** Mixing alcohol with certain common medications, such as aspirin, acetaminophen (Tylenol), and ulcer medications can cause the BAC to rise more rapidly.

Prolonged alcohol consumption can lead to physical tolerance, as your brain becomes accustomed to a certain level of alcohol. You need to consume more alcohol to achieve the desired effects. This could lead to abuse and alcoholism.

■ Alcoholism

Alcoholism is a chronic disease with genetic, physiologic, and psychosocial consequences. Like other addictions, alcoholism is characterized by the following: drinking more alcohol than intended; persistent desire but unsuccessful attempts to stop drinking; frequent withdrawal and absenteeism; decreased performance at school or work; continued drinking despite the realization that his or her drinking is causing physical, social, or psychological problems; the presence of withdrawal symptoms when not drinking; and the need for increasing amounts of alcohol to achieve intoxication.

Drinking Responsibly

Abuse of alcohol is no longer the cultural norm, even in many segments of the college student population. Responsible drinking is always up to you. Alcohol does not need to be present to have a good time with friends. However, if you choose to drink alcohol, it is imperative that you also eat, to slow the rate of alcohol absorption into your body. Set a limit in advance on how many drinks you are going to have, and stick to it. Always go to a party with a designated driver, a friend who, in advance, commits to not drinking. Do everything possible to prevent an intoxicated friend from driving.

Don't rely on alcohol or other drugs as a means to relax; find alternative measures such as exercise, listening to music, reading, meditation, yoga, guided imagery, biofeedback, and hobbies to help you unwind.

Finally, don't drink alcohol just because you observe others drinking or because you believe "everyone else is doing it." According to national surveys, more students **believe** that others are using alcohol (95 percent) than what is actually reported (85 percent). Students who choose not to drink excessively report "second-hand" effects of the irresponsible use of alcohol by their friends. These non-drinking students are more likely to be physically abused or assaulted by their drinking friends, or become a victim to sexual harassment or assault. Academic performance may also suffer because of time spent caring for a roommate who had too much to drink; decreased study time, lack of sleep, and poor concentration may also be "second-hand" effects when friends or roommates drink irresponsibly.

Using Campus Resources

The health center on most campuses sponsors student organizations which provide information and consultations concerning alcohol and drug abuse prevention. BACCHUS (Boost Alcohol Consciousness Concerning the Health of University Students) is a national student organization that provides programs on responsible alcohol use, including National Collegiate Alcohol Awareness Week and the Safe Spring Break campaign. To find out more information, contact your campus health center or counseling center. They may have physicians or mental health professionals who can assist you or refer you to a community organization for treatment.

HIV Infection and AIDS

We are experiencing an epidemic in the United States that is actually a worldwide pandemic. Infection with the Human Immunodeficiency Virus (HIV) has become the number-one challenging public health problem today, with far-reaching medical and psychosocial consequences. It is estimated that over 30 million people worldwide are infected with HIV, with approximately 16,000 new infections occurring daily. In the United States, it is estimated that over one million people are living with HIV infection, with about one-third having Acquired Immunodeficiency Syndrome (AIDS), the terminal phase of the continuum of HIV infection. States with the highest incidence of HIV and AIDS are California, New York, Florida, and New Jersey. The incidence of HIV infection is highest in individuals between the ages of 20 and 29 years, with the incidence of AIDS highest during the fourth decade of life (i.e., between 30 and 39 years of age). In the United States, AIDS is now the second leading cause of death among people aged 25 to 44, and in many parts of the country, AIDS is now the number-one cause of death among men in this same age range. Although the rate of infection is still highest in men, the incidence of infection is steadily rising in women. HIV infection is disproportionately higher among African Americans and Hispanics, when compared to Caucasians.

■ Epidemiology

The Human Immunodeficiency Virus is difficult to acquire. It is not spread through respiratory droplets or through casual contact, like the common cold or influenza viruses. You cannot acquire HIV by touching, simple kissing, hugging, or sitting next to someone who has the infection. HIV is not transmitted by sharing eating utensils, handshakes, using toilet seats, donating blood, or by mosquitoes.

There are only a few modes of HIV transmission. The virus is present in significant amounts only in blood, semen, vaginal secretions, and breast milk. The virus is present in very small concentrations in saliva, but there is essentially no risk of transmission via deep kissing. Transmission of HIV can occur as a result of:

- **Sexual activity.** HIV can be spread in semen and vaginal fluids during unprotected anal, vaginal, and oral sexual contact with an infected partner. Transmission is more likely to occur during anal intercourse than vaginal intercourse, and more likely to occur during vaginal intercourse than oral sex. Women are more likely to acquire HIV from an infected male partner than are men acquiring HIV infection from a female partner. The largest number of cases (55 percent) of HIV transmission involves homosexual sex, usually unprotected anal intercourse, between men; however, the incidence of heterosexual transmission has risen steadily over the past seven years, and is currently at 18 percent.
- **Injections using shared needles.** Any contaminated needle can transmit the virus, making steroid use, tattoos, and body piercing potentially risky unless sterile needles are used.
- **Perinatally.** A baby may **acquire** the virus before birth via the mother's circulation through the placenta, during the birth process via vaginal secretions, or after birth via infected breast milk. Mothers who are HIV positive have a 25 percent chance of infecting their unborn baby; this number decreases to less than 10 percent if the mother receives treatment during pregnancy.
- **Transfusions of blood, blood products, or organ transplants from HIV-infected individuals.** Since March 1985, the blood supply has been tested for the presence of HIV, significantly decreasing the incidence of HIV transmission via this means. Changes in the methods of screening blood donors have also helped with this decline. However, the risk still is present albeit very small.

■ Testing for HIV

The most widely used tests to determine the presence of HIV infection actually do not detect the virus itself, but measure the presence of antibodies that are formed in response to infection with HIV. The standard laboratory blood tests that are most commonly used are the Enzyme Linked Immunoassay (ELISA) and the Western Blot. The Ora-Sure is a type of ELISA test that detects the presence of HIV antibody in the mouth mucosa rather than in the blood; the accuracy of the Ora-Sure test is about the same as for the blood test.

- *Always use a latex condom rather than a natural membrane condom.*

- *Store condoms in a cool, dry place; never store them in the car or in your wallet.*

- *Do not use condoms beyond their expiration date.*

- *Only use water-based lubricants, such as K-Y Jelly; oil-based lubricants will break down the latex.*

- *Use spermicide containing nonoxynol-9, as this compound inactivates HIV.*

- *Know how to use a condom properly; practice if necessary.*

- *Do not reuse a condom.*

- *ALWAYS use one!*

Figure 4 ■ Guidelines for Condom Use

The Western Blot is a more specific and expensive test and is therefore primarily used as a confirmatory test when the ELISA comes back as positive. The Western Blot is performed on the same blood specimen which resulted in the positive ELISA. If the ELISA is positive and the Western Blot is negative, the person does not have HIV infection. If the ELISA and the confirmatory Western Blot tests are both positive, then the person is diagnosed as having the HIV infection.

Since it takes at least two weeks to six months for the body to produce enough HIV antibodies to be measured by the tests, a negative result obtained on a test done too soon after the last risky behavior may not be accurate. It is imperative, therefore, that the ELISA be performed at least one additional time, preferably about six months later. Approximately 95 percent of people who have been infected with HIV will have positive blood tests within the first six months.

Anyone who feels they may be at risk should be tested for HIV. Early testing is important because treatments with AZT, ddI, ddC, and the powerful protease inhibitors suppress proliferation of HIV and, in most cases, lower the number of viruses in the bloodstream to undetectable levels, leading to a delay in the onset of AIDS symptoms. The use of AZT and the protease inhibitors, however, does not represent a cure. To date, there is no cure for HIV, and education remains the key ingredient in prevention.

■ Limit Your Risk

NO ONE IS IMMUNE! Your risk of acquiring HIV infection is not dependent on who you are, but is dependent on your behaviors. The only absolutely safe way to protect yourself is by reducing or eliminating risky behaviors. If you do choose, for example, to have sexual intercourse, you should ALWAYS use a condom, even if you think that your partner is not infected. You can never be certain of your partner's past sexual history or drug use history, because he or she may have acquired HIV from a previous partner several years ago. Unknown to both of you, your partner may have slept with someone who slept with someone who once secretly abused injection drugs. Remember, once individuals become infected with HIV, they can remain completely asymptomatic for many years and may not even know that they have the infection! Next to abstinence, the safest way to protect yourself is to always use a latex condom with the spermicide nonoxynol-9. How confident do you feel that you will practice safer sex? Complete Exercise 2 to find out.

■ Summary

We discussed several important ways to enable you to live a balanced, healthy life. Health is something to be cherished. A healthy student is one who will excel academically, be more productive, and have time to pursue recreational pursuits and spend quality time with family and friends. A healthier student is a happier student, a happier employee, and a happier member of the community. Healthy decision making while in college will pay big dividends, with many benefits that will last far after you graduate.

■ Exercise 1. Wellness Lifestyle Assessment

DIRECTIONS: Using the following scale, answer each statement by placing the number that most closely corresponds to your lifestyle and feelings in the space preceding each statement.

KEY: 1 = "no/never" or "don't know"
2 = "rarely" or "1–6 times a year"
3 = "occasionally" or "1–4 times a month"
4 = "often, frequently" or "2–5 times a week"
5 = "yes/always" or "almost daily"

A. Physical Assessment

_____ 1. I perform aerobic exercises for twenty minutes or more per session.

_____ 2. When participating in physical activities, I include stretching and flexibility exercises.

_____ 3. My body fat composition is appropriate for my gender. (Men: 10–18 percent; Women: 16–25 percent)

_____ 4. I have appropriate medical checkups regularly and keep records of test results.

_____ 5. I practice safer sex or abstinence. I never have sex when intoxicated.

B. Nutritional Assessment

_____ 1. I eat at least 3 to 5 servings of vegetables and 2 to 4 servings of fruits daily.

_____ 2. I eat at least 6 to 11 servings daily of foods from the bread, cereal, rice, and pasta group.

_____ 3. I choose or prepare foods that tend to be lower in cholesterol and saturated fat.

_____ 4. When purchasing foods, I read the "Nutrition Facts" labels.

_____ 5. I avoid adding salt to my food.

C. Alcohol and Drugs Assessment

_____ 1. I avoid smoking and using smokeless tobacco products.

_____ 2. I avoid drinking alcohol or limit my daily alcohol intake to two drinks or less.

_____ 3. I do not drive after drinking alcohol or after taking medications that make me sleepy.

_____ 4. I follow directions when taking both prescription and over-the-counter medications.

_____ 5. I keep a record of drugs to which I am allergic in my wallet or purse.

D. Emotional Wellness Assessment

———— 1. I feel positive about myself and my life. I set realistic goals for myself.

———— 2. I can effectively cope with life's ups and downs in a healthy manner.

———— 3. I do not tend to be nervous, impatient, or under a high amount of stress.

———— 4. I can express my feelings of anger.

———— 5. When working under pressure, I stay calm and am not easily distracted.

E. Intellectual Wellness Assessment

———— 1. I seek advice when I am uncertain or uncomfortable with a recommended treatment.

———— 2. I ask about the risks, benefits, and medical necessity of all medical tests and procedures.

———— 3. I keep informed of the latest trends and information concerning health matters.

———— 4. I feel comfortable about talking to my doctor.

———— 5. I know the guidelines for practicing good preventive ~~medicine~~ and self-care.

F. Social and Spiritual Wellness Assessment

———— 1. I am able to develop close, intimate relationships.

———— 2. I am involved in school and/or community activities.

———— 3. I have recreational hobbies and do something fun just for myself at least once a week.

———— 4. I know what my values and beliefs are and I am tolerant of the beliefs of others.

———— 5. My life has meaning and direction. I have life goals. Personal reflection is important.

■ Analyzing Your Wellness Assessment

For each of the six wellness sections, add the total number of points that you assigned to each question. Place the totals of each section below:

TOTALS for each of the six sections:

A. Physical Assessment   _____

B. Nutritional Assessment   _____

C. Alcohol and Drugs Assessment   _____

D. Emotional Wellness Assessment   _____

E. Intellectual Wellness Assessment   _____

F. Social and Spiritual Wellness Assessment   _____

TOTAL POINTS   _____

Then, divide the Total Points by six to get the
"Average Wellness Score" =

What do your results mean? The results apply to each of the six individual sections, as well as for determining your overall wellness assessment (after dividing your total score by six).

Total for each section (or Average Wellness Score)	RESULTS (for each individual section and for the overall assessment)
23–25	Excellent Your lifestyle choices and attitudes can significantly contribute to a healthy life. You are to be commended!
19–22	Good You engage in many health-promoting behaviors and attitudes. You care about your health. However, there are some areas that you could improve to provide optimal health benefits and wellness.
11–18	Average You are typical of the average American who tends to not always practice the healthiest of behaviors, despite having the knowledge which would suggest the contrary. Now is the time to consider making changes in your lifestyle to foster a healthier future.
5–10	Needs immediate improvement You are to be commended for being concerned enough about your health to take this assessment, but your behaviors and attitudes may be having a detrimental effect on your overall health. Now is the time to take action to improve your health!

■ Exercise 2. Can You Practice Safer Sex?

Most people know how HIV is transmitted and what behaviors are necessary to reduce their risk of acquiring the virus. However, some of these behaviors are not always easy to do. Your confidence in yourself to perform these protective sex behaviors is as important as simply knowing what the behaviors are. Assess your safer sex confidence level by answering these questions honestly, according to the key below:

KEY: A = I always could do this in all situations.

B = I could do this occasionally.

C = I could not do this.

_____ buy condoms at a store.

_____ discuss using a condom with a new sex partner before having sex.

_____ refuse to have sex with a person if he or she did not want to use a condom.

_____ talk to a new sex partner about his or her past sexual experiences and number of sexual partners.

_____ ask a new sex partner whether he or she has ever had sex with another person of the same sex.

_____ ask a potential sex partner about the use of intravenous drugs and sharing of needles.

_____ be able to avoid using alcohol on a date to help make a decision about sex easier.

_____ be able to clearly express what my sexual expectations and limits are before beginning any sexual activity.

_____ be able to resist an unwanted sexual advance or stop sexual activity if a condom wasn't available.

_____ be able to resist an unwanted sexual activity even when slightly intoxicated after a few drinks.

What do my results mean?

1) Multiply the number of responses you answered with "C" by 2.
2) Add to the result, the number of responses you answered with "B."
3) Responses answered with "A" do not count as points.
4) Add the answers from 1) + 2) above to get the "Confidence Score."
5) Circle your overall confidence score on the continuum below to determine your risk.

0	2	4	6	8	10	12	14	16	18	20

LOW RISK   HIGH RISK

If you scored between 10 and 20 points, you tend to doubt your ability to behave in a way that would protect you from acquiring HIV. You should evaluate your own beliefs and attitudes concerning safer sex in the four areas assessed: condom use, self-protection, sex under the influence, and sexual limits.

CHAPTER 3 DIVERSITY
Living in a World of Diversity

Introduction

If you live and attended high school in a small, suburban or rural community, you may be encountering more diversity at your community college than you've ever seen in your life. If you are from an urban environment, you may find your campus has more, less, or about the same amount of diversity that you are used to. Whichever the case may be, your future will include living, working and doing business with people from all walks of life. They may be from different racial/ethnic/cultural groups, practice different religions, have different social or economic status, speak different languages, be different ages, have physical/mental disabilities, have different sexual orientations, or work/be training for jobs that are not traditionally held by people of that gender. The ability to cooperate and work effectively with all types of people is an important skill that you need to develop in order to be successful in today's world.

Pretest

Answer yes or no to the following items:

	Yes	No
1. It is easier for minority students to get financial aid to attend college.		
2. Discrimination against women and minorities in the workplace is a thing of the past.		
3. The large middle class in the U.S. controls most of the nation's wealth.		
4. Gay men/lesbian women are attracted to all members of the same sex.		
5. Latino people don't want to learn English.		
6. Victims of domestic abuse would leave their abuser if they really wanted to.		
7. Asian students have higher GPA's than students of other cultural groups.		
8. Older people are less productive in the workplace.		
9. Homeless people could easily change their situation if they tried.		
10. It is unlikely that I (or a member of my immediate family) will become disabled.		

You may have noticed that all of the items on this pretest are false. They represent some commonly held beliefs that are based on stereotypes rather than facts. In this chapter we will take a closer look at some of the myths about diversity as we arm you with some truths. You will read about the population of the United States and how it is changing. We will discuss the big three diversity issues—race, social class, and gender—that have been part of the historical legacy of discrimination in this country. Then, we will consider some of the newer issues such as ability, age, and other forms of prejudice. Finally, we will talk about some ways to manage living and working in such a diverse society: understanding intercultural communication patterns, deciding what is fair, and showing respect and acceptance for our fellow human beings.

■ The American Population

The Way It Was

When we look at the United States today we see the results of hundreds of years of history. Who runs the country politically and economically, who gets along with whom, what actions receive what kinds of reactions all come from the foundations that were laid when this nation was formed.

Aside from the Native Americans and Mexicans (a blend of Native Americans, Spanish, and Africans), most people coming to the New World were from the countries of northern and western Europe. At the time of the American Revolution, there was also a considerable population of people brought from Africa as slaves. In the 1800's immigrants from China, who came to work on the railroads, were populating the Pacific coast states, especially California. By the early 1900's, the migration of people from western Europe gave way to an influx of immigrants from eastern and southern Europe.

As each new group of "foreigners" entered the country in large numbers, they were a concern for those already established here. Fears that the new immigrants would take their jobs, intermarry with their children, speak languages they didn't understand, practice different religions, and bring strange, "un-American" ways of doing things to their communities fueled feelings of "us" versus "them." Newcomers were often unwelcome in established neighborhoods, and ethnic areas sprang up in most cities. In the late 1800's and early 1900's, laws were passed to limit the number of "undesirable" immigrants, such as the Chinese and Japanese, from entering the country. Many of these laws were not repealed until the mid-1960's.

Slavery was yet another matter. Although the slaves were freed after the Civil War, extreme prejudice and fear led many states and communities to pass laws that systematically discriminated against people of color, especially Blacks. It was illegal for slaves to be educated or own property, and even after slavery ended, they were often denied opportunities and rights that were taken for granted by other citizens.

The Way It Is

This history still affects all of us living in the United States today. The legacy of discrimination persists, and thus, we find ourselves dealing with problems in the 21st century that had their roots in the 17th, 18th, 19th and 20th centuries. One of the critical issues facing our nation today is whether we will be able to solve our dilemma concerning diversity. School curricula have long ignored the contributions of people of color in the sciences, math, history, literature, the arts, etc. Consequently, generations of Americans have grown up thinking that most of the knowledge of the world has come from white European cultures. This promotes feelings of superiority among some Euro-Americans.

The white majority has also controlled governments and the court systems at the local, state, and federal levels. Those in power influence the kinds of laws that are passed, the way they are interpreted, and the way they are enforced. Issues such as racial profiling and hate crimes dominate the news, signifying that Americans still struggle with how to get along. Terrorism is on the rise and has directly affected our country, resulting in fear, negative attitudes, and violent acts against innocent people who are targeted just because they come from the same ethnic background as the suspected terrorists. The problem will not go away by itself; indeed, it is far too important to ignore.

The Way It Will Be

There is no doubt that the population of the United States is getting more diverse. The 2000 census revealed some major demographic shifts in our country. For all of our nation's history, the dominant group numerically, politically, and economically has been Americans of European decent, most of whom classify themselves as "White, Non-Hispanic." In the next 100 years this will change. Predictions based on previous and current U.S. census data indicate that the number of White, Non-Hispanic people will steadily decrease each decade of this century. Sometime between 2055 and 2060, there will be a break-even point where the number of White, Non-Hispanics will fall to 50% of the total population. By the end of the 22nd century, they will comprise about 40% of the population.

At the same time, the number of Hispanics will continue to increase. They were the second largest minority group throughout the 1990's, with slightly under 12% of the population in the 2000 census. By 2100, Hispanics are expected to become a third of the total population. Blacks, at 12.1% in the 2000 census, have previously been the largest minority group in the U.S. Their population is expected to stay very stable for the next hundred years, increasing to about 13% of the population at the end of the century.

Another group that is expected to grow rapidly is the Asian/Pacific Islanders. They comprised fewer than 4% of the population in 2000. Their numbers are expected to grow consistently each decade throughout this century, by the end of which they will almost match the number of Blacks living in the U.S. These projections are illustrated in the following table:

Percent of Total Population								
	2000	2010	2020	2030	2040	2050	2075	2100
White Non-Hispanic	71.4	67.3	63.8	60.1	56.3	52.8	45.6	40.3
Hispanic	11.8	14.6	17.0	19.4	21.9	24.3	29.5	33.3
Black Non-Hispanic	12.2	12.5	12.8	13.0	13.1	13.2	13.2	13.0
Asian/ Pacific Islander	3.9	4.8	5.7	6.7	7.8	8.9	11.0	12.6
American Indian	0.7	0.8	0.8	0.8	0.8	0.8	0.8	0.7

Source: Projections of the Resident Population by Race, Hispanic Origin and Nativity, U.S. Census Bureau, Population Division, Washington, D.C.

[The United States conducts a census of all citizens and residents living in the country every ten years. The categories above are those identified in the 2000 census. Further information can be obtained from the Census Bureau website at www.census.gov.]

Implications for Change

If you are in your late teens and twenties and live into your 80's, which is quite likely given the advances in health care, you will see this shift in population in your lifetime. But we don't have to wait that long to confront the issues that such diversity will bring. Each new development in technology—radio, telephones, television, air travel, satellites, computers—brought the people of the world closer together. The introduction of the Internet cemented the relationship among us as customers in a global marketplace. Time and distance have lost their ability to control trade or productivity. Any possibility of isolationism on the part of the United States ended early in the 20th century. International business is the norm, whether you are on the plains of central Iowa, the tundra of northern Alaska, the beaches of Florida, or in a major metropolitan area.

How can we deal with the rest of the world, though, when we have not yet mastered the ability to get along with our fellow citizens? In the cities and states where demographic shifts have already taken place, people struggle with accepting differences. Many fear change. Others fear that people who look "different" will harm them or take away their quality of life. Some individuals/groups do not want to give up their privileges (or perceived privileges) so that others who are not part of their group may benefit.

Although these thoughts and feelings are kept under control most of the time, one incident is often all it takes for old prejudices and stereotypes to surface.

■ The Big Three: Race, Class, and Gender

The concepts included in any discussion about diversity can be many and varied, but the three major areas of concern have always been, and still are, race, social class, and gender. Let's take a look at each one.

The Question of Race

How many races do you think there really are? If your answer is more than one, we all have a problem. How did this notion that there is more than one race, the human race, come into existence? Biologically/genetically, human beings are all of the same species. Regardless of skin/eye/hair color, language spoken, religion practiced, or cultural background, we can give each other our blood, transplant organs from one person to another, reproduce offspring, etc. So, what purpose do you think it served to create a system that divided people into separate races? Who gained and who lost with such a system? Why do we perpetuate this type of classification? Why does racism (especially between Blacks and Whites) continue to be one of the nation's most prevalent social problems 150 years after slavery ended?

What do you think will happen when there is no longer one clear majority group? Will we all truly be equal then? Will we finally be able to overcome the divisiveness caused by years of living in a system that classifies people by certain physical characteristics? Where do you stand on this issue?

If you identify yourself as a member of the White race, you are already in the smallest minority of people populating the earth. Does it bother you that within your lifetime, and certainly that of your children, the white population will be a minority in the United States? Are you able to live and work comfortably with the diversity of people around you? Do you understand that you benefit daily from unearned privilege just because of your skin color, and can you understand the frustration of those who have not been granted that same privilege?

If you consider yourself Hispanic or Latino, you are in one of the fastest growing groups worldwide. Historically, your group has always been underrepresented politically in the United States because many Latinos do not vote or get involved with politics. Male and female Latino students drop out of high school at much higher rates than their peers. Latinas (females) are among those least likely to attend college and finish a degree. Are you prepared to step up and take your place in society? Do you plan to finish college, earn a professional degree, and make sure that your children do the same?

If you are Black or African-American, you are living out the legacy that your parents and grandparents fought to achieve. Their sacrifices and persistence in the face of overwhelming obstacles earned you the right to attend the college of your choice, to shop in any store, to eat in whatever restaurant you choose, and to work alongside other Americans. Yet, their fear is that you will sit back complaisantly and stop the progress for which their generation worked so hard. They fear that you will give in to the myth that to be intelligent and accomplished in anything except music or sports is to "sell out" or "act white." Are you committed to stopping the cycle of poverty and hopelessness that fills the inner cities of America?

If you identify yourself as Asian/Pacific Islander, you may not see as many people in the United States with your physical features, but you are in the largest population group in the world. The prevailing stereotype is that all Asian Americans are "A" students and are good in math, science, and computers. It is true that for many years, U.S. immigration policies primarily allowed scientists, doctors, and technologists to come to this country, and it is also true that in many Asian families, education is highly valued and doing homework is a top priority. However, for those of you who excel in athletics, social sciences, or fine arts, it may be frustrating not to be given the opportunity to do your thing because you are expected to be a math whiz or computer geek. As your population increases in the U.S., you should gain more visibility in all areas: government, media, athletics, business, etc. Are you fulfilling your personal goals and being true to yourself?

Many Americans do not identify with any of the groups listed above. A "multiracial" classification was added to the census for the first time in 2000. That made it easier for people with multiple heritages to feel included. (Counting and classifying has come a long way from the first census where the only choices were "White" and "Non-White.") Most Americans of Middle Eastern descent identify themselves as White because there is no category that accurately describes them. Native Americans must prove that they are at least 1/16 blood-related to a specific tribe in order to legally claim that heritage. Assigning a racial identity to people is a tricky undertaking at best. Perhaps the real solution to the question of race is to view yourself as a member of the human race. Then, you will see the differences between human beings as being surface variations among your neighbors, friends, and family.

Social Class

One characteristic that has made the United States such a great nation is that most of the population is middle class. We don't have a large peasant class ruled by an aristocracy or a select group of military leaders. However, in the last half of the 20th century some of the progress made by the middle class has been lost. Although the per capita income of Americans has increased, when the figures were adjusted for inflation, there was actually a decline in quality of life and income of the middle and lower classes. The gains reflect an increase in the incomes of the upper class. If we were to illustrate the distribution of wealth in the United States, it would look like an inverted pyramid with the wealthiest 10% of the population controlling 80% of the country's monetary resources. So, the rich really are getting richer, and the poor are getting poorer.

This is a cause for concern for all classes because the middle class is the only one that cannot pass its class status to the next generation. Children of upper class parents can inherit the family fortune and remain in the upper class. Poor parents have little material wealth to leave their children, which often leads to multi-generational poverty. That's why the middle class has always valued education as its primary means of holding on to its position or getting ahead. If children of middle class parents do not have sufficient skills to get good jobs and succeed on their own after reaching adulthood, they will not be able to maintain middle class status without support. With a few exceptions, education level is directly related to income level. Statistically, people with higher levels of education also earn higher levels of income.

With an increase in income level and social class comes better access to health care and thus, longer life expectancy. The opportunities available to you are also affected by income. Even personal safety is determined to some extent by where you can afford to live. In this country your quality of life is greatly determined by your socio-economic status.

The good news is there was a slight decrease in the number of people and families living in poverty in the United States in 2000. The United States Census Bureau calculates the poverty index by comparing a family's income to its size. People whose household income is less than the threshold for the size of their family are said to be living in poverty. The poverty threshold for a family of four in 2000 was $17,463, and for an individual under the age of 65, it was $8,959.

The bad news is that poverty continues to be a reality for many, even in one of the wealthiest nations on earth. Race/ethnicity is still a major factor in determining who is poor. The following chart shows the percentage of people living below the poverty level in the United States in the year 2000 according to the Census Bureau.

Race/Ethnicity	% Living in Poverty
All races	11.3
White Non-Hispanics	7.5
Blacks	22.1
Hispanics	21.2
Asian/Pacific Islander	10.8

Poverty is also highly related to marital status and gender. Single women with children are much more likely to be poor than married couples with children, single men with children, or unrelated individuals. Look at the same chart that includes poverty levels of families in general and those headed by single females with children. Do you see the dramatic increase in poverty levels for single mothers and children?

% of People Living Below the Poverty Level			
Race/Ethnicity	All People	People in Families	Single Mothers and Children
All Races	11.3	9.6	27.9
White Non-Hispanics	7.5	5.5	18.0
Blacks	22.1	20.8	38.7
Hispanics	21.2	20.1	36.5
Asian/Pacific Islander	10.8	9.5	19.5

Source: Historical Poverty Tables, U.S. Census Bureau

One of the newest faces of poverty in the 21st century is that of the young child. Homeless families now outnumber homeless singles. According to the National Coalition for the Homeless, families are the fastest growing segment of the homeless population. Over 1.2 million U.S. children are homeless on any given night, and 41% of these children are under the age of 5. The average age of the homeless population is 9 years old! What future consequences will there be on education, job training, and work-related issues for these young people? Over half of them switch schools at least two times during the year, and almost a fourth must repeat a grade because of it.

Poverty and homelessness go hand in hand. The federal government defines affordable housing as being about 30% of a person's income. Under that guideline, a minimum wage worker would have to work more than 80 hours per week in order to pay rent on the average 2-bedroom apartment. For those whose income is not sufficient to pay for food, childcare, health care, education, and housing, the latter is often the one that gets sacrificed or forfeited. Many people, even in the middle class, are living from paycheck to paycheck. An accident, major illness, or other unplanned expense is all it would take for them to lose their home.

The more factors you have working against you, the harder it is to become successful in American society. Because public schools are usually funded by property tax revenue, those located in poor areas lack the resources of their more affluent neighbors. They cannot afford the best teachers, equipment, or supplies. New technology is limited or sometimes even nonexistent. Graduates of these schools may be as intelligent and have as much or more potential to learn, but may score lower on achievement tests than their peers who have benefited from numerous advantages. Consequently, they may not be accepted into the best colleges/universities or offered the same opportunities for career advancement. For years our society has struggled with how to make life more equitable and just for those whose school and/or life experiences have not prepared them adequately. Affirmative action, busing, and other such programs have tried to bridge the gap, but are often criticized as being unfair or falsely held to cause reverse racism and/or classism.

The federal government created financial aid programs to help people in the low and middle economic classes to be able to afford college. Post secondary education (college or vocational/skills training) that prepares students for careers paying decent wages is the most cost effective way to help people get out or stay out of poverty. It may seem like minority students get financial aid at disproportionate rates compared to white students, but the facts show that minority students are more likely to come from families living below the poverty level. That explains why they are more likely to get government grants that are based on family income. The government does not request or require an applicant to indicate race or ethnicity on the FAFSA (Free Application for Federal Student Aid) forms. Privately funded scholarships do exist for minority students, but their numbers are not even close to the numbers of scholarships awarded to white students.

Gender

Historically, the first discrimination was probably between men and women. This phenomenon was already present at the beginning of our great nation. It is evidenced in the preamble of the Constitution of the United States, when our forefathers emphasized that all men were created equal. That is literally what they meant—all **men**. (However, remember that in 1776 all men really meant all white, educated, male property owners.) The inequity was also evidenced by the more than 140 years it took women to finally get the right to vote and hold public office. This second-class status is socialized within the very fabric of our nation and its people. We are still trying to overcome the notion that women are the weaker gender.

It is very apparent when one looks at the inequities found within careers and salaries. If you take women in business as an example, we find that less than five women are Chief Executive Officers of Fortune 500 companies (the 500 companies that make the most money in the U.S.). That means the other 99% of CEO's are men. Males still make more money than women for the same jobs with the same educational level. Even though it is illegal to actively discriminate in this manner, it is still practiced. It is carefully concealed, but in jobs where there is not a straight scale, where negotiation is part of the starting salary process, men negotiate better deals than women. Why? It could be that women lack the confidence to drive the hard bargain, or it could be due to the person who does the hiring. More often than not the person in charge of personnel selection is a man.

Even today when we know that most single parent families are headed by women, and in most two-parent families both spouses work outside the home, there is still the perception that men are the "breadwinners," and therefore, should earn more. Think of how many men you know that feel threatened when their wife's salary is higher than their own. Are they proud of her, or do they feel intimidated? How many couples would move to a new city because the wife was offered a better job?

Yet, although they earn less, women pay more for goods and services. When women buy cars, they pay inflated prices compared to men. They are charged more for services such as dry cleaning clothes, alterations, haircuts, and car or home repairs. Women are also more likely to be victims of domestic violence and physical assault. Many women stay in abusive relationships out of fear, and because they lack alternative means to support themselves and their children. Anti-stalking laws and orders of protection do not prevent women from becoming victims. These laws can only be enforced after a crime has been committed.

In government we still see inequities between men and women despite all of our progress. Today there are four or five governors, thirteen United States Senators, and two women on the Supreme Court. However, since women make up 51% of the population, that's still gross under-representation. Women win elections at about the same rate as men when neither is an incumbent (person currently doing the job). Male or female incumbents win elections at a much higher rate than challengers. The few women in elected positions show, not that people won't elect women, but that women are still playing catch up for all the years they were prevented from holding such a position. There are far more male incumbents today because there have always been more males in office.

In the career arena we find that the major professions traditionally held by women do not have the earning power of male dominated occupations. I've heard the argument that women tend to work at less demanding, less difficult occupations; that their jobs take less skill and expertise than male dominated occupations. Is it really true that the person who cares for your child or teaches your child to read is worth less per hour than the person who unclogs your sink? In almost every occupation, though, you will find a wage gap between men's and women's salaries. The August 2001 issue of *Working Women* lists the differences in average salaries for men and women in the same occupations. Here are some examples from their 2001 Salary Survey:

Profession	Women	Men
Accountant	$ 36,263	$ 44,115
Radiologist	$240,982	$365,783
University professor	$ 61,933	$ 65,152
Elementary school teacher	$ 35,050	$ 43,000
Secretary	$ 22,500	$ 32,400
Registered nurse	$ 39,100	$ 44,500
Pediatrician	$126,891	$150,876
Real estate salesperson	$ 29,250	$ 44,500
Electrical Engineer	$ 77,400	$ 83,300

What do you see when you look at these comparisons? We could try to explain this by saying that men have worked longer in these occupations, and therefore, have more experience. But that won't explain why men in traditionally female occupations such as secretaries, nurses, and elementary school teachers still have higher salaries.

Sometimes the issues are not as obvious. Bias can be found in something as subtle as providing less funding for medical research to cure breast cancer or other "women's diseases." It can be a teacher giving the girls in class less encouragement to pursue higher levels of math and science. In fact, studies done by Drs. David and Myra Sadker showed that elementary and secondary school teachers gave more instruction and attention to the boys in their classes than the girls, even when the teachers were aware that they were being studied and were trying to be equitable. Girls were praised more often for their appearance and the neatness of their work. If they made mistakes, they were told that they were incorrect, but not given further instruction. Boys in the same classrooms were praised more for the quality of their work, and when they made mistakes, they were retaught the concept.

The Sadkers also studied the students' self-concepts. They found that girls had higher self-concepts and expectations of success than boys in elementary school and junior high, but by the time they reached high school, the boys far outpaced the girls in those same areas. They concluded that the socialization process still tells girls that there are limits to what they can achieve, and that it's not feminine to be smart in science, math, technology, and/or the skilled trades.

■ Diversity Issues Today

We've come a long way toward acknowledging that prejudice and injustice stifled the opportunities of many Americans in the past. Making the connection between that historical legacy and current problems is more difficult for many students to see. However, we live in an age of international businesses where companies are bought and merged with others across continents, and chances are you will work for and with people who are very different from you. If you can't get along in a diverse workforce, you will find your employment opportunities severely limited. It is time for each of us to confront our own attitudes and beliefs. Ask yourself, "How well will I be able to cope if my boss and/or co-workers speak another language, practice a different religion, come from a 'foreign' culture, have a different sexual orientation, are much older/younger than I, or are disabled?"

Ability

How do you react when you see someone in a wheelchair? Do you ignore them or look away? Do you think of them as less intelligent? If they are with a companion, do you speak to the person directly or to the companion? Do you act like they are also hard of hearing or cannot speak? These are common reactions that people with disabilities experience constantly. Only as recently as 1990 has there been a federal law giving those with disabilities a chance for equal opportunities. If you have ever had to use crutches or a wheelchair for a period of time, you might have a slight appreciation for what persons with physical disabilities experience on a daily basis. Trying to do normal activities such as use public restrooms, sit in a theater, board an airplane, train, or bus, shop for groceries, or attend a sporting event can be quite an ordeal. As an able bodied person, do you resent having to walk farther because the parking spaces closest to the door are designated handicapped? Do you step aside or use the stairs when a person in a wheelchair is waiting to get on a crowded elevator?

What if the disability is not obvious? What about someone with a learning disability? Do you think it is a waste of taxpayer money to fund special tutorial programs for L.D. students? What if you are the person with the learning disability? Many students with learning disabilities have had to endure years of suffering because parents, teachers, and classmates didn't understand or accommodate their disability. Schools today try to do a better job identifying these students at an early age, but if you are an adult, you may not have been so fortunate.

Our culture seems to value people according to two main criteria: physical attractiveness (beauty/youth) and intelligence. In his book *Hide or Seek*, psychologist Dr. James Dobson calls them the gold and silver coins of self worth. Those people blessed with the golden coin of beauty don't have a problem finding friends and getting positive attention from others. From the time they are cute babies through their high school years where appearance is the key to popularity, they seem to draw people in with their good looks and charming smiles. Those with the silver coin, intelligence, may not be as popular as their golden classmates, but they, too, are recognized as possessing something of great value. Their parents and teachers are proud of them, they win awards, and they feel good about themselves and what they can accomplish.

Let's turn the picture over, though, and look at some of the other children. Imagine a child with a learning disability who cannot understand the lessons the way the teacher explains them. S/he receives no awards for outstanding performance, even though s/he may put forth much greater effort to learn. What is done to rescue the self-esteem of this student? The child with a physical disability is often made to feel less than adequate in a society that worships perfection. Do we contribute to these problems with our perceptions of people with disabilities? Do we limit the things we think they can accomplish?

This is another area where we might really need to make some adjustments in our thinking. Sometimes life has a way of forcing us to rethink and adjust our attitudes. People who are able bodied and perfectly healthy one day can, through an accident or illness, become disabled in a matter of minutes. Your chance of developing some type of disability in your lifetime is 50/50, and the percentage increases as you age. What will you do then? Will you give up on life, or will you continue to achieve and perhaps even excel?

We have many examples of people who have overcome even extreme disabilities and accomplished great feats. Some have done more with their lives because of their disability than they would have had they stayed able bodied. One example is a woman named Joni Erickson Tada. As a result of a diving accident when she was a teenager, Joni became a quadriplegic who has no control over her body from the neck down. During rehabilitation therapy she learned to draw and paint by holding the paintbrush with her teeth. After she became well known for her art, she decided to tell her story in a book. That was the beginning. Today, she has written several books, has had two movies made about her life, has become an international authority and advocate for the disabled, is invited to speak at conferences around the world, runs her own charitable corporation, and has a daily radio program.

We can all probably think of someone who has not let a physical or learning disability keep them from achieving success. Some of the greatest scientists, musicians, artists, entertainers, politicians, and athletes have had to overcome seemingly impossible odds to accomplish their goals.

Age

Ageism has been around for quite a while, but it is receiving considerable attention now that the baby boom generation is getting older. Advances in health care have enabled people to be productive into their later years. Many choose to continue working in their careers because they find their work stimulating and satisfying. Some pursue a new career after retirement to keep themselves busy and active. On the other hand, the economic situation of many older Americans is what keeps them in the workforce. They simply cannot afford to retire.

At the same time, our workplaces are changing. Technology, information, and innovations are constantly forcing companies to keep up. They seek younger, energetic workers who can deal with constant change and who are knowledgeable about the latest technology. Older workers can find themselves devalued and pushed aside. As a culture and as individuals, we seem to have lost respect for our elders. We're too busy to sit and talk with them and learn from their wisdom. Their slowness irritates us if it interferes with our faster pace.

However, those companies that do take advantage of hiring seniors find that they are excellent employees. Most were raised in a time when you had to have a good work ethic. They are experienced, dependable, hardworking, honest, and can save the company money because their absentee rate is much lower than younger workers, while their punctuality rate is much higher.

Of course, ageism can go the other way, too. Sometimes teenagers are the targets of negative stereotyping. Because of the widespread negative publicity about teens who commit crimes, people get the impression that all young people are lazy, selfish, troubled and confused. The reverse is closer to the real truth. Teens today are doing better than previous generations in many ways.

Other "Isms" That Separate Us

Another step on our journey toward making this nation a more perfect union of people is to rid ourselves of the "isms." We've taken a look at the big three—racism, classism, and sexism. We've also discussed discrimination against people with disabilities and ageism. Unfortunately, there are still more dragons out there to slay. So, pick up your sword, and let's go get them!

What are some of the "isms" you've encountered? You may not be able to label them with snappy, one-word descriptions, but you know when you've observed or experienced them. Perhaps it is prejudice because of religious beliefs. What about discrimination based on a person's size? Have you ever noticed how people treat someone (especially a woman) who is very large, or someone (especially a man) who is very short? Those who don't fit the "norm" are likely to be ridiculed and rejected for being different.

Cases involving harassment and discrimination against homosexuals have made news headlines in recent years. Homophobia, an extreme prejudice against gay men and/or lesbian women, causes those who fear homosexuals to act out against them. Behaviors ranging from "practical jokes" to violent assaults or defamation violate the victim's civil rights and are inappropriate in any setting. Many corporations and municipalities have adopted policies aimed at protecting employees and preventing discrimination based on sexual orientation.

People with alternative lifestyles are a part of your campus and your community. Your campus may have a gay/lesbian club or organization. Gay/lesbian students are entitled to the same rights and considerations as all other persons on campus. You will encounter people with different lifestyles wherever people are found—in the workplace, in your neighborhood, within organizations to which you belong, in your place of worship, etc.

Whenever we put another person into a category labeled "other" or "not like us," it increases the chances that we will treat them differently than we would like to be treated. It makes it easier to rationalize away behavior that we would immediately recognize as wrong if it happened to someone in our family. Watch for other examples of the "isms" as you interact with people. Then, resolve to become part of the solution, not part of the problem. Be an advocate for justice, fairness, and equity through your own words and actions.

■ Managing Workplace Diversity

Intercultural Communication

Every encounter with another person is an intercultural exchange. We each see the world with perceptions developed from our own experiences. We've each developed a communication style that serves our needs. Misunderstandings arise, though, when our style clashes with another person's communication style. We think they are being emotional and unprofessional. They think we are cold and don't care enough about important issues. Suddenly there is a problem. What is the answer to dealing with people who are different when we all have to get along?

Dr. Milton Bennett has identified several sets of factors that make up a person's communication style. First, recognize your own style, and then watch for these elements when you communicate with others. Recognizing that there are style differences can help you tune in to what your co-worker is really trying to say. For example, some people get right to the point when they talk. They might fill in a few details later, but the "bottom line" is what communication means to them. For other people, the context and the details are essential, and from there the listener can figure out the main point. To them it is condescending to spell everything out as you would to a young child. Imagine what happens in a business meeting where the participants have opposing styles. One person is thinking, "Why does s/he talk in circles? I don't need all of this information. This is a waste of time." The other person is thinking, "Does s/he think I'm stupid? Why won't s/he trust me with all of the details?"

In Western cultures, communication tends to be very direct. You have probably heard someone say, "I just tell it like it is." Saying exactly what you're thinking, without worrying about whether or not the circumstances and timing are perfect is an approach many Americans use regularly. However, people in several Eastern cultures find directness rude and insulting, especially if the news is bad. They may favor a more indirect style where meaning is conveyed through nonverbal behavior and implications. Indirect communicators may make statements within earshot of a person rather than address the comment directly to that person. This allows the listener to hear the message but is far less confrontational.

Another difference in the way people communicate has to do with how much they depend on words and how much they say through nonverbal messages. Some people are very good at "reading between the lines," while others take everything that is said at face value. Men and women often have this style difference in personal relationships. She thinks he should understand without being told. Her internal dialogue says, "If he was observant, he would know." His internal dialogue says, "That's ridiculous. How am I supposed to know what she wants if she doesn't tell me?"

Communicating clearly is extremely important in the business world where profits are made or lost by the way employees interact with customers and each other. Corporations spend millions of dollars on conflict resolution training. Many times this training involves personality testing that helps people understand themselves and their patterns of interacting. Recognizing that people have different personality types and communication styles makes one aware of how to interpret another's way of expressing him/herself. As you talk with others on the job, at school, and in your personal life, try not to judge them or be offended if they don't respond the way you expect, but rather approach the situation with an open mind. Different isn't necessarily better or worse, it's just different.

Deciding What Is "Fair"

How does an individual or an employer know which is the right way to proceed when making decisions that involve diversity? How can you be sure that you are being just or fair in your treatment of others? There are two ways of approaching the issue. Both have merit and work in many situations. Read through the two descriptions and decide which you favor instinctively. Then consider the other approach and think about the positives and negatives of using that. Be objective and open minded; think of situations when it might be better to switch from your preference to the other point of view.

The first approach is systematic and rule-based. One establishes policies and procedures for doing things and then follows them closely. Decisions are made by adhering to specific guidelines. Everyone is treated the same because the standards are the same for all. Companies with policies that apply to every employee from the entry-level workers to the executives are practicing this kind of fairness. If your community college uses a placement test, the same cut off scores should apply to all students. Parents who want to be fair often try to treat their children the same. If they buy something for one child, they buy something of equal value for the other children.

The second approach is not as rigid in its application. Sometimes following the rules too closely gets in the way of what makes sense in the situation. Taking extenuating circumstances into account and treating each person as an individual ensures fairness. Schools that have zero tolerance policies for drugs and weapons are under fire for suspending students who give a friend an aspirin or accidentally leave a butter knife in their car. Companies may make an exception to a tardiness rule if an employee was late due to an auto accident on the way to work. Most parents wouldn't think of buying glasses for all of their children just because one child needed them, or buying glasses for one child and gifts of equal value for the others.

In many situations you will be faced with deciding what is the best way to respond. Is it fairer to hold to the standard, or is it better to look at the unique circumstances and do what is best in the situation? When dealing with diversity, sometimes the second approach makes more sense. We are not all the same. We do not all have the same advantages or disadvantages. Isn't true fairness doing what is appropriate to ensure that all have an opportunity to succeed? A culturally sensitive person will look for clues and cues about what works and how others prefer to be treated. There is not an instant answer; it may take time and effort to develop your intercultural skills.

Respect and Acceptance

In recent years we have seen people do terrible things to one another because they can't deal with their differences. How do we help people process their anger over dealing with someone who is different?

Many diversity programs emphasize tolerance. If we are all going to live and work together, we have to move beyond tolerance. One of the most positive ways to ensure workplace harmony is for us to treat each other with respect and acceptance. Recognize that we are better off with our differences than we would be apart. Diversity isn't about others; it's about all of us.

If you struggle with issues of diversity, try the following tips for becoming a more open and accepting person.

- *Develop a sense of community.* When you interact with people in a friendly environment, you begin to feel part of the group. It is easier to support and understand someone with whom you have established a rapport or relationship. At work or at school, try to eat lunch or take breaks with fellow employees/students whose backgrounds differ from yours.
- *Travel or participate in cultural exchanges.* This can give you the most amazing change of perspective. Seeing/hearing news reports from another country's press alerts you to the cultural bias in our own media. Meeting and talking with people on their "turf" helps you see things from their point of view.
- *Learn another language/learn about another culture.* Knowledge is power. If you lack knowledge about other cultures, take a cultural diversity course. Many colleges/ universities require at least one course from a different cultural perspective as a graduation requirement. Knowing a second language not only helps you communicate with people, but it is also a window into their culture.
- *Practice cultural humility.* Your own way of doing things may not always be the only way, the right way, or even the best way.

■ Summary

Even though we would like to think that every individual in the United States has an equal opportunity to achieve and succeed, the facts do not support that assumption. Some have a much greater head start. Factors such as parental levels of education and income, individual talent and skill, educational background, and opportunities/experiences contribute to a person's chance for success.

In this chapter we have explored a few of the many concepts of diversity. The changing population of the United States and the globalization of our economy will force Americans to deal with people who are different in a just and equitable way. We considered the three biggest categories of diversity: race, social class, and gender and how each of them has disadvantaged many persons in our society. The new issues: ability, age, homophobia, and other "isms" were also discussed. To manage workplace diversity, learn how you communicate and understand that others may use a different style. Treat those you encounter with respect and acceptance.

"The end result of a discussion on ethnicity should be to increase and celebrate it—that's diversity. The end result of a discussion on race should be to decrease the impact of it—that's unity."

—Dr. Milton Bennett

■ Journal Assignment

Choose one of the following topics and write in your journal about it:

1. Think about an incident of discrimination or harassment that you experienced or witnessed. (The discrimination may have been based on race, ethnic group, religion, sex, physical disability, or age.) How did the experience affect you and the other persons involved? Discuss your feelings, values, beliefs, and actions after the incident. What actions can you take to reduce the occurrence of such incidents?

2. Reflect upon sex discrimination in our society. How has it affected you or a person who is important to you (e.g., your spouse, child, friend, or relative)? Write about the effect of sex discrimination on self-esteem, education, career choices, relationships, and leisure activities. What are your feelings about sex discrimination?

3. Write about the experience of someone you know who has a physical or learning disability. How has that person coped with the challenges of daily life, pursuing his or her education, participating in leisure activities, establishing a social life, or finding a job?

4. If you are a non-traditional student (more than 25 years of age), write about the persons who have supported and encouraged you to attend and succeed in college (e.g., your family, a mentor, a friend) or your own inner strength and motivation. What additional resources might you tap to help you succeed in college? How have you coped with the challenge of juggling the many roles in your life in addition to your role as a student? How do you feel about being an older student on campus?

5. If you are a traditional college student (less than 25 years of age), write about your experiences with non-traditional students. How have they enhanced your college education? Are there any disadvantages to having non-traditional students on campus?

■ Homework Activity

Suppose you have to write a research paper for a sociology class. The paper has to be about diversity in America.

Step 1   Narrow your topic by choosing a specific diversity concept to research. Write it here:

_____

Step 2   Use the computerized card catalog system (such as Illinet Online) in your college's library/LRC and locate one reference book that you could use for your paper.

Name of book _____

Author(s) _____

Call number _____

Step 3   Using one of the periodical databases, identify three journal/magazine articles that would help you gather information for your paper. Print an abstract of each article and attach it to this page or copy down the full citation.

Article 1 _____

_____

_____

Article 2 _____

_____

_____

Article 3 _____

_____

_____

Step 4   Read one of the articles and be prepared to give a brief summary of it in class.

CHAPTER 4 TIME MANAGEMENT
Taming Time

It's a sad but true fact that much of your success or failure in college (and probably the factor that you can control the most) depends directly on how you manage your time. Even though it is such an important factor to master, it is probable that most of us have developed our "time management plan" simply by habit and not by devising a workable action plan. Have you ever stopped to consider that time is one thing in life that can never be saved? It can only be spent, and unfortunately, too many of us have developed the skill of wasting time to a fine art! We may value many things and possessions in life, yet if we had all the money in the world we could not buy one hour. Maybe we should examine this valuable commodity a little more closely!

From *Practical Approaches for Building Study Skills and Vocabulary,* Second Edition by Funk et al. © 1996 by Kendall/Hunt Publishing Company.

■ Why Is Time Management So Crucial?

In high school, it was quite possible to waste fairly large amounts of time without dire consequences. Teachers and parents seemed to give you the benefit of the doubt and understand that you needed some leeway in your time. Even if you've been away from school, you've probably avoided assignments with due dates. But in college, your responsibilities seem to be multiplying in and out of the classroom, and the same habits of "time-waste" will soon catch up with you—possibly with unpleasant results! Many students learn this sad fact too late. Four of the major reasons for dropping out of college have been listed as economic reasons, personal reasons, academic reasons, and lack of organization skills, according to Diana Scharf Hunt—co-author of *Studying Smart: Time Management for College Students.* This lack of organization coupled with a tougher academic load means that time management suddenly becomes (or should become!) a high priority for college students if they are going to be one of the survivors. And that's not even taking into consideration that most college students want to spend some of their time participating in the vast amount of social life available or hold jobs.

Consider the possibility that all of these potential problems can be removed or prevented by the simple realization and acceptance that we frustrate ourselves by trying to control what we can't, and failing to control what we can. Time is the one thing we can never increase. But we can certainly increase our management of it by devising a plan—a workable, personalized, motivating, structuring plan.

■ What's the Most Important Thing to Learn in College?

Nothing else will be learned unless you learn to control your management of the time available to you. You either control time, or it (or the lack of it) controls you. You must decide. We all have 24 hours in a day—86,400 seconds—to fill up. How do you fill up yours?

Activity:

Take a minute or two to begin filling in "The Week that Was" time schedule. Record what you have accomplished so far today. List your classes, sleeping and eating time, visiting time, dressing time, work time, and, oh yes, your study time! What if this pattern continues for the rest of the week? Continue to record what you do for one week as accurately as possible. Have you controlled time, or did it manipulate you? After you have completed the worksheet, fill in the final portion by analyzing the hours you have spent the past week doing the major necessities of college life—classes, studying, sleeping, eating, and working. Subtract your total from the total amount of hours available in a week, and then divide that by seven to get a daily amount. You may be amazed at the amount of time you waste, or at least fill up with a multitude of things that are not very important.

■ Where Did It Go?

In a recent study at Southwest Missouri State University, students analyzed their time with these shocking results:

Time spent weekly in class—13 hours
Time spent studying—15 hours
Time spent sleeping—45 hours
Time spent eating—11 hours
Work hours (if they had jobs)—16 hours
Total hours used up—84–100 hours (depending on whether they had a job)
Total hours in a week—168 hours
*Total hours unaccounted for—68–84 hours

That's from 10–14 hours a day! Where does all of that time go? Of course, outside jobs take up some time, and errands, and visiting, and family obligations, etc. . . . But do you have 10 hours today with nothing specific to do? Of course not! No one has that kind of free time—or do they? Is it possible that it's there, and we just can't see it?

For example, did you know that the average American spends seven hours a day watching TV? Even if we said that estimate was much too high and lowered it to 25 hours of TV viewing weekly, that would be 10 years of the average 70-year life—[1/7] of your life in front of a machine! Yet in this same study, the average American only spent 19 minutes daily in active conversation, 13 minutes in hobbies, five minutes in enjoying sports, and four minutes daily in book-reading. These statistics would seem to point to the fact that Americans value TV viewing above all other pastimes, but the study concluded by the participants expressing that they value the other possibilities much more highly than TV. Maybe lack of time is not the problem; maybe it's lack of direction and planning!

The haphazard and careless use of time does at first seem to be much easier and less complicated, but it returns very poor investment dividends. Being organized and controlling your time is much easier in the long run, and less stressful! Remember the value of working smarter, not harder.

■ Okay, How Do You Control Time?

There are three easy steps in learning to control your time. First, you must have a goal, or you have no purpose to plan. We have discussed the vital importance of goals earlier in this book, but keep in mind that without a goal, you will not know when you have arrived! Secondly, you must formulate a plan to reach that goal—a step-by-step way to get where you want to go. Finally, you must attack your plan and take action. Unfortunately, that's where most of our plans go awry. This is the hardest part, to just get started. We can usually finish if we can just get started! Thomas Huxley once said, "Perhaps the most valuable result of all education is the ability to make yourself do the thing you have to do, when it ought to be done, whether you like it or not." To control time you must take charge of your time by planning your priorities and devising a way to deal with them—one step at a time.

The only way you will ever be able to gain control of your busy schedule is by learning two very simple guidelines.

1. You must learn to do your jobs as efficiently as possible so that they take the least amount of time and still produce the quality of work desired.

2. You must learn to use the small blocks of time usually wasted.

Efficiency experts are frequently hired by large corporations to teach their workers how to produce the most in the least amount of time. Studying should be approached no differently. There are many ways to study more efficiently. Future chapters will provide you some of these ways. As for the second guideline, this is where the 10–14 "lost" hours go for most people—hidden in 18 minute, 10 minute, and four minute intervals. We conveniently convince ourselves that we cannot start, work on, or finish a job now, because we "don't have time." Most projects for busy, productive people cannot be started and finished in one neat, tidy package. It takes distributing the work load in order to finish the task. And that's why you need a time schedule!

■ What's the Benefit of a Time Schedule?

We'll give you several!

1. *A time schedule saves time.* It takes time to devise a schedule, but it saves time in the long run. This works in much the same way that following a map saves time when traveling. Now you can get from here to there without a map, but it's much more efficient and less stressful to decide on the best route and then follow it!

2. *A time schedule will separate work and play.* It will not rigidly control your life as you may fear, but scheduling will help provide order and discipline. This will free you to work when you work and play when you play. One of the most stressful aspects of college life is that the work never seems to be done. As one chapter is completed, another is assigned. What's the advantage of taking a test when you just have to start studying for another? If you are going to enjoy your college career and also be successful at it, you must learn to separate work and play. If you don't, your work will not be as efficient as it should be and your play will not be as enjoyable as it could be!

3. *Time schedules reduce the amount of time wasted.* Whether you choose to waste it or not, time has a way of evaporating quickly! For example, did you know that you will spend six months of your life waiting at stop signs? How do you feel about spending eight months of your life opening junk mail, or one whole year looking for lost items? And then there are those five years of waiting in line. If you are going to waste time, you should do the deciding about when to waste it!

4. *Scheduling time helps to decrease your "slacking off" periods.* Most humans tend to slack off in their work habits and productivity near the end of the day, the week, the semester, and so forth. If you plan your schedule you can help to prevent this, or even accommodate this tendency by utilizing your "prime time." This is that time when you are at your peak efficiency and when you can accomplish the most. You won't need to feel guilty about slacking off if you have already achieved your projected plan.

5. *Time schedules help prevent cramming.* If the only benefit of a time schedule was that it helped to prevent cramming and thus promote retention of learning, we feel it would be worth it! Research after research proves the benefit of distributing your study times into several periods rather than one massive period of torture the night before the test or assignment. Not only will you remember more with this spacing out of studying, but your health and emotional well-being will have a better chance to prosper. Physically as well as academically, cramming does not pay! Just as a path in the woods is more easily seen if traveled over several times, material is more easily recalled if rehearsed at different sessions.

6. *A time schedule helps to promote balance in your life*—a balance of work, study, recreation, and free time. You need breaks as you study (10 minutes for every hour or so is a good rule of thumb), and you need recreation to re-create your body, soul, and spirit. If your balance of life gets out of whack, it is hard to enjoy any aspect of it fully.

7. *Scheduling helps daily chores get accomplished.* By planning it out, maybe you could find a way to manage those chores that seem to get out of hand so easily—things like getting the dishes or the laundry done, writing to your family, or even paying the bills. Schedule a time when you will take care of these little-but-necessary jobs, and half the work is done.

8. *Are you too busy?* One of the greatest benefits of a schedule may be to find out if you CAN get all this stuff done! You may be asking too much of yourself. It simply may not be realistic to work 32 hours a week and take 19 credit hours, plus raise two children (or find time for two boyfriends—whichever fits your situation)! You may find that you must drop certain activities, combine projects, reduce the frequency of events, or alternate weeks in order to live sanely.

9. *Time schedules help you to overcome the worst hurdle of all—getting started!* We tend to avoid the doing of disliked tasks, or substitute doing jobs that are less important, but more appealing. We procrastinate to the best of our ability if it suits our purpose or mood for the moment.

■ The Problem with Procrastination

If we could learn to solve this problem, most of our time worries would be solved. For most college students, procrastination is the worst academic problem they face, except for the problem of remembering what they have learned. Procrastination seems to be the main cause of anxiety and worry in the overall picture—we could have done a better job and been less stressed out if we had just had more time to do the job! And we could have had more time if we had started the job before the last minute. Procrastination means needlessly postponing tasks until later, and it is really just a strategy that people use to protect themselves from certain fears. These fears usually involve the fear of failing, or even succeeding! Statements like: "I must be perfect," "It's safer to do nothing than do the wrong thing," or "If I do a good job, I may have to do an even better job next time" are common thoughts for procrastinators. Many of us probably fall into this category if we are honest with ourselves. Overcoming procrastination is a matter of habit and will-power, and the only way to cure the problem is to face the fears. Setting daily goals, prioritizing, breaking the job into small, easily-accomplished sub-parts, setting time limits, and rewarding yourself for an accomplished task may help you with the procrastination problem.

■ How Do You Make a Time Schedule?

You will first need to consider what type of time schedule or schedules will best suit your purposes. There are daily schedules, weekly schedules, or semester schedules, and you may need one or all of these. As a suggested minimum, you will need a semester calendar, an average weekly master plan, and a daily list. If you want the maximum of efficiency, you need to incorporate all three types of schedules.

The Semester Calendar

As soon as you get your different class syllabi for a new semester, you should fill out as much of a semester calendar as you can. Plot test dates, due dates, (VACATION DATES!), and begin to develop an overall scheme of busy weeks versus planning weeks. You might even plot in notes to yourself like "Start worrying about term paper topic" or "Two tests coming up in two weeks" on your calendar at the appropriate locations. You will begin to feel a little more in control as soon as your calendar is in shape. Now all you have to do is plan on how to accomplish the week-by-week tasks.

The Weekly Master Plan

Let's now work on making a weekly schedule for an average week in your current semester. On the Master Time Schedule provided, you should first schedule in the names of the classes you are taking. Attending class may not be your only "job" right now, but it should certainly be a very high priority if you are going to be successful in college. In a very real aspect, attending class is your career right now. Do it professionally!

Secondly, go back through the time schedule and list those demands on your time that do not vary that much from week to week. You might call this "Necessary Time." It would include such things as outside jobs, eating, sleeping, clubs, sports, practices, commuting time, church, housekeeping chores, etc.

After having filled in CLASS TIME and NECESSARY TIME, you are now ready to figure out STUDY TIME. In order to accomplish this task, you should first analyze your study time from "The Week That Was" Time Schedule you filled out. Take a minute to complete the Time Analyzer Worksheet before you go any further and then decide how you measure up. You should try to remediate problems that you are giving yourself by your study behavior. Remember, your goal is to study smarter, not harder. The step of deciding WHAT to study WHEN will be one of the most important decisions you will make this semester. We'll look at this carefully in the next section.

Finally, the blank spaces that will remain in your time schedule after you fill in your study time will be your FREE TIME. We usually can find plenty of ways to fill in these blanks as the days go by. We've provided you with an extra copy of a Master Schedule so you can make more copies as the need arises. Use it! The problem that must now be dealt with is how to schedule that study time.

▪ How Do I Decide When to Study?

In the first place, you need to decide how much time is needed for study. In high school, 15–30 minutes per class was usually sufficient, but those days are gone! Usually a 2/1 ratio is suggested—that is, two hours of study for every hour of class time. So a very general rule would be that if you were carrying 15 credit hours, you should find 30 hours of study time. Of course, some classes might not require this, but some may require more. It is much wiser to plan too much time and not need it than to not plan enough and find out too late just how badly it was needed! Usually a one hour study session with a ten minute break could be a workable goal for most students. You would need to adapt this to what is most productive for you; 30- or 45-minute slots with five minute breaks might be more beneficial.

As to how to pick the most productive time to study each subject, consider these guidelines.

1. The OPTIMUM TIME for the most efficiency is usually RIGHT AFTER THE CLASS. To study the subject right BEFORE THE CLASS meets can be very advantageous for discussion classes, or even just a quick review of notes before a lecture can make those classes more beneficial. To pick a time slot right after class can increase your efficiency and decrease the time needed to study. For example, a 30-minute study immediately after class could be worth one hour of study later. You tend to be more

interested in the subject at that time, need less warm-up time to get involved in the studying, and there tends to be less confusion about assignments if they are started quickly.

2. Try planning a time to REVIEW your notes immediately BEFORE YOU GO TO SLEEP. Plan on learning new material when you are fresh, but review right before you retire. Studies have shown that you retain this reviewed material better if you sleep on it. In fact, the shorter the delay between study and bed, the more likely you are to retain the material!

3. Plan on studying your MOST DIFFICULT CLASSES IN THE EARLY AFTERNOON, for the most part. Long-term memory seems to be more effective then, as well as hand-eye coordination and physical strength. If you need to memorize or juggle words or figures, your short-term memory is more effective in the morning, so plan those types of activities for earlier hours. Beware of general low-energy time zones— for most people these center around 2–5 pm (when neural functions decline and blood sugar levels are lower) or 2–7 am (when most accidents that can be attributed to human error occur). These might not be the optimum times to write that difficult research paper.

4. FOLLOW YOUR BIOLOGICAL CLOCK. Find your prime times and work with your body rather than fighting against its natural tendencies. To find whether you are a night person (an owl) or a morning person (a lark), take the inventory and then plan to study for tests at your peak periods. Morning people tend to jump out of bed early in the morning with a drive to have a productive morning. They tend to lead controlled, structured, well-regulated lives. They begin to slow down about mid-afternoon and believe and follow the old adage of "Early to bed, early to rise . . ."

On the other hand, night people (or owls) crawl rather than jump out of bed, barely survive mornings, begin to wake up about noon and become their normally extroverted selves, peak in mid-afternoon, and wind down quite a bit later. No one tendency is the correct one, but you must work with your preference or it will defeat you. Don't plan on getting up early and cramming for the big final if you are a night owl. You probably won't make it up! And if you are a morning lark, you'd better not go ahead and attend the big party with lofty plans to study all night long. Your body won't make things easy for you to follow through with your plans. Consider these factors when you schedule classes.

One final thought about your body's biological clock is that most people tend to find benefit in keeping in step with the sun. There seems to be some added benefits to working during daylight hours and resting during night hours.

5. Make sure you SPACE YOUR STUDYING PROPERLY. Remember to plan and use breaks that vary greatly from what your study activity was. Alternate different types of study activities. For example, plan to study an activity subject (such as math or composition) between subjects that require a lot of reading. And make sure you space out the studying required for each subject. It will usually be more effective to study biology in three one-half hour sessions rather than one and one-half hour session. Don't forget to include a time to review past notes also. Otherwise, you will be practically starting over when it is time for testing.

6. DOUBLE TIME ESTIMATES AS YOU PLAN. Things always seem to take longer than originally thought. In fact, you need to guard against "Parkinson's Law"— work always stretches to fill whatever time is available. Instead of planning on studying one hour, plan how much you will get accomplished in one hour. Set goals and limits and you will be able to achieve more.

7. Plan to STUDY EACH SUBJECT AT THE SAME TIME, ON THE SAME DAYS, AND IN THE SAME PLACE (one place with everything you need close at hand). Again, the idea is to work with your body instead of against it, and you can condition your body to not resist studying so much if you establish very firm habits. If you have psychology on Mondays, Wednesdays, and Fridays, the best time to study would be on those days at whatever time you designate would fit your biological clock, your time schedule, and be closest to psychology class time.

8. In general, plan to study the WORST FIRST, EASIEST (OR MORE INTERESTING) LAST. Prioritize, and then plan on getting the tough stuff over while your energy and initiative are at their peaks.

■ What about "Daily" Time Management?

As you try to follow your weekly Master Time Schedule, you will also need to make daily plans. A good suggestion is to make out this daily plan before you go to bed at night. Although it takes time and energy, devising a list of what you would like to accomplish the next day will help give you direction and purpose, and start your day more efficiently. But one more step is needed—prioritize that list before you start sawing logs. That way if you don't get everything done you will at least have accomplished the most important things. Try making some copies of the Daily Plan Worksheet we've provided, and see if it doesn't help you to put life into perspective and order. You're beginning to get a grip on it!

Critical Thinking

Take a minute to look back on yesterday's events. Write down all the things that you did yesterday—in the order that you did them. Analyze your accomplishments. Did you think about the priority of the task as you started to work? Did you really accomplish the things that needed to be taken care of yesterday? Would there have been a better order to have worked on those tasks, or should some tasks have been omitted and others substituted? Try prioritizing yesterday's events now in the light of a new day. If you had worked in this order yesterday, would today's tasks be any easier or more organized? Keep this activity in mind as you think about whether to make a list and prioritize it for tomorrow!

■ Any Other Time Management Tips?

Sure! Take a look at these:

1. Make studying as portable as possible. Carry pocket work/note cards to study when you are on the go.

2. Use those small blocks of time usually wasted. Recite, review, and plan in-between classes, while waiting in lines, etc. Carry a small notepad to help you plan.

3. Make lists and prioritize them. This idea paid one man (efficiency expert Ivy Lee) $25,000 and made Bethlehem Steel Company and Charles Schwab, its president, a hundred million dollars! Lee instructed each steel worker to make a list each day, prioritize the list, and then work on the first item until it was done. Then, and only then, they were to move on to the second item. This strategy turned that little known company into the biggest independent steel producer in the world. The idea was simple then, and is still simply effective now—take things one at a time in their proper order.

4. Recognize four things that will steal more time from you than you can make up for—laziness, sidetracks, procrastination, and day-dreaming. These things must constantly be fought.

5. Use calendars, clocks, appointment books, and notepads to their full advantage by planning ahead, organizing, and following the plan.

6. Try to handle each task only once. Finish the job as much as your schedule will allow before proceeding to the next task.

7. Practice trading time, not stealing it. Has an unexpected social event popped up? Go ahead and attend guilt-free—as long as you trade the study time you had planned for free time later in your schedule. Don't just put it off—plan and trade it.

8. Learn to say no, and mean it.

9. Control interruptions.

10. Avoid perfectionism. Shoot for your best, but don't overdo this time-sapper.

11. Plan, and then start! Remember: the more time spent planning, the less time needed to accomplish the task. When it's time to start the task, throw yourself into it with enthusiasm. Don't wait for inspiration to strike. It probably won't. Don't inch into the water—dive in! Genuine enthusiasm may follow!

■ Mastering the Time Trap

Now that you know why to do it, and how to do it, let's do it! Devise your master time schedule and diligently attempt to follow it. You may soon find that there are a lot of benefits in being the master OF—rather than being mastered BY—your time. You can win in the game of time if you learn what the worn-out, frustrated student in this example learned:

"I can't keep our appointment," he sighed. "I find myself swamped. It's getting to be too much!"

"You've contracted a malady about as unique as the common cold," replied his friend. "It's called Wrong Ending. You know, we were all given two ends to use. On one we sit, with one we muse. Success depends on which we use . . . heads you win, tails you lose."

One final comment—don't forget the importance of balance in your life. Does your time schedule have a balance of work and play, study and recreation? Get your life too much out of balance in either direction and you are asking for trouble. You're on your way to a bright future if you learn the secret of mastering your time! And what a secret to learn, for the waste of time is one price winners can't afford to pay!

■ Summary

In this chapter we have discussed the fact that it is critical to master time management in college in order to succeed academically AND socially. College students are very busy people with places to go, family obligations, people to see, and tests for which to study! None of these things can happen efficiently unless one learns to control the balance of work and play in his life. Effective people must also learn to work out a manageable way to arrange their schedule so that they are making the best use of the time they have. Lack of time is really not the problem; procrastination and poor planning are the real culprits. We learn to control time by devising and learning to follow a time schedule that takes into consideration our schedules, goals, priorities, and biological make-up. The benefits of this planning device are numerous, including distributing the work load and helping to reduce stress. This chapter has given you an opportunity to make a time schedule and suggestions for choosing your optimum study times. There are ways to make time management more efficient and effective, and the suggestions included in the last section of the chapter should give you some positive steps to take in the right direction!

Name: _____ Date: _____

■ "The Week That Was": Your Current Time Schedule

	Monday	Tuesday	Wednesday	Thursday	Friday	Saturday	Sunday
6:00 A.M.							
7:00 A.M.							
8:00 A.M.							
9:00 A.M.							
10:00 A.M.							
11:00 A.M.							
NOON							
1:00 P.M.							
2:00 P.M.							
3:00 P.M.							
4:00 P.M.							
5:00 P.M.							
6:00 P.M.							
7:00 P.M.							
8:00 P.M.							
9:00 P.M.							
10:00 P.M.							
11:00 P.M.							
MIDNIGHT							
1:00 A.M.							
2:00 A.M.							

Totals:

Hours Spent in Class   _____   168   (total hours in 1 week)

Hours Spent Studying   _____ – _____   (your total of "necessary hours")

Hours Spent Sleeping   _____   _____   (hours unaccounted for weekly)

Hours Spent Eating   _____

Hours Spent Working   _____   7 $\overline{}$ (hours unaccounted for PER DAY!)

Total   _____

◼ Time Analyzer for "The Week That Was" Worksheet

Analyze your current time usage by answering these questions based on what is normal for you.

	YES	NO
1. I often study at a time when I am not at peak efficiency due to fatigue.	____	____
2. I have failed to complete at least one assignment on time this semester.	____	____
3. This week I spent time watching TV, visiting, or napping that really should have been spent otherwise.	____	____
4. Often, lack of prioritizing tasks causes me some difficulty in completing tasks on time.	____	____
5. Social or athletic events cause me to neglect academic work fairly often.	____	____
6. At least once this semester, I have not remembered that an assignment was due until the night before.	____	____
7. I often get behind in one course due to having to work on another.	____	____
8. I usually wait until the night before the due date to start assignments.	____	____
9. My studying is often a hit-or-miss strategy which is dependent on my mood.	____	____
10. I normally wait until test time to read texts and/or review lecture notes.	____	____
11. I often have the sinking realization that there is simply not enough time left to accomplish the assignment or study sufficiently for the test.	____	____
12. Often I rationalize that very few people will make the A/get the project done on time/really read the text, etc.	____	____
13. I catch myself looking forward to study interruptions rather than trying to avoid them.	____	____
14. I have failed to eliminate some time wasters this past week that I could have controlled.	____	____
15. I often feel out of control in respect to time.	____	____
16. I have procrastinated at least twice this week.	____	____
17. I find myself doing easier or more interesting tasks first, even if they are not as important.	____	____
18. I feel I have wasted quite a lot of time—again—this week.	____	____
19. I studied EACH course I am currently taking this week.	____	____
20. I spent some time this week reviewing previous weeks' notes even though I did not have a test.	____	____
21. The time of day that I am the most alert is _____ , so I tried to study my hardest subjects then.	____	____

	YES	NO

22. I studied approximately 1–2 hours out of class for every hour in class.   _____ _____

23. My most sluggish period during the day is _____ , so I used these times to relax or participate in sports or hobbies.   _____ _____

24. I often make out daily lists of tasks to be completed, and I prioritize these lists.   _____ _____

25. I use small blocks of time (10–30 min.) between classes to review notes, start assignments, or plan.   _____ _____

To calculate your score, score 1 point for each yes from items 1–18, and 1 point for each no from items 19–25. The higher your score, the more you need a Master Time Schedule! Consider these categories for your score:

15–19 YOU'RE IN DESPERATE NEED OF A PLAN! How do you ever get anything accomplished? (Or do you?)

10–14 YOU NEED A PLAN! Life could be simpler if you took the time to plan it out.

5–9 A PLAN WOULD HELP! The going could be smoother, and more could be accomplished.

0–4 A PLAN COULDN'T HURT! You're doing pretty well, but give yourself the gift of organization, and you may give yourself the gift of more time.

Please write a paragraph that reflects on your results.

_____

_____

_____

_____

_____

_____

_____

_____

_____

_____

_____

Name: _____ Date: _____

■ Master Time Schedule

	Monday	Tuesday	Wednesday	Thursday	Friday	Saturday	Sunday
6:00 A.M.							
7:00 A.M.							
8:00 A.M.							
9:00 A.M.							
10:00 A.M.							
11:00 A.M.							
NOON							
1:00 P.M.							
2:00 P.M.							
3:00 P.M.							
4:00 P.M.							
5:00 P.M.							
6:00 P.M.							
7:00 P.M.							
8:00 P.M.							
9:00 P.M.							
10:00 P.M.							
11:00 P.M.							
MIDNIGHT							
1:00 A.M.							
2:00 A.M.							

Name: _____   Date: _____

■ Master Time Schedule

	Monday	Tuesday	Wednesday	Thursday	Friday	Saturday	Sunday
6:00 A.M.							
7:00 A.M.							
8:00 A.M.							
9:00 A.M.							
10:00 A.M.							
11:00 A.M.							
NOON							
1:00 P.M.							
2:00 P.M.							
3:00 P.M.							
4:00 P.M.							
5:00 P.M.							
6:00 P.M.							
7:00 P.M.							
8:00 P.M.							
9:00 P.M.							
10:00 P.M.							
11:00 P.M.							
MIDNIGHT							
1:00 A.M.							
2:00 A.M.							

■ Morning Lark vs. Night Owl

This questionnaire can help you determine if you are a morning person (a lark) or a night person (an owl). "Larks" usually lead well-structured, controlled lives. They jump out of bed and usually have productive mornings, tending to wind down about mid-afternoon. "Owls," on the other hand, tend to crawl out of bed, barely live through mornings, but have more productive afternoons. They also tend to be more extroverted than larks. Which are you? Find out by circling the answer most appropriate for you and adding up your points.

	Points Possible	Points Earned
1. I feel best if I get up around:		_____
5–6:30 am	5	
6:30–7:30 am	4	
7:30–9:30 am	3	
9:30–11 am	2	
11–noon	1	
2 If I had to describe how easy it is for me to get up in the morning, I would say:		_____
It is not easy at all!	1	
It is not very easy.	2	
It is fairly easy.	3	
It is very easy.	4	
3. The way I feel for the first half-hour after I wake up is:		_____
very tired	1	
fairly tired	2	
fairly refreshed	3	
very refreshed	4	
4. If I could choose the best time to take a difficult test, it would be:		_____
8–10 am	4	
10 am–1 pm	3	
1–5 pm	2	
7–9 pm	1	
5. If my job would require that I work from 4–6 am one day, I would choose to:		_____
not go to bed until after I worked	1	
take a nap before and sleep after	2	
sleep before work and nap after	3	
get all the sleep I need before work	4	

	Points Possible	Points Earned
6. If someone asked me to jog with them at 7 am one morning, I would perform:		_____
well	4	
reasonably well	3	
not very well	2	
not well at all	1	
7. If I have to wake up at a specific time each morning, I depend on my alarm clock:		_____
not at all	4	
slightly	3	
quite a lot	2	
desperately	1	
8. I am usually tired and wanting to go to bed by:		_____
8–9 pm	5	
9–10:30 pm	4	
10:30 pm–12:30 am	3	
12:30–2 am	2	
2–3 am	1	

TOTAL NUMBER OF POINTS EARNED

A score of 20 is halfway between owl and lark. The higher your score, the more of a morning lark you are. The lower your score, the more of a night owl you are.

Name: _____ Date: _____

◼ Daily Plan for _____
(Date)

Jobs to Complete	Due Date	Priority	Completed?
1. _____			
2. _____			
3. _____			
4. _____			
5. _____			
6. _____			
7. _____			
8. _____			
9. _____			
10. _____			

Phone Calls to Make			
1. _____			
2. _____			
3. _____			
4. _____			

Errands to Run	Due Date	Priority	Completed?
1.			
2.			
3.			
4.			
5.			
6.			

People to See			
1.			
2.			
3.			
4.			

Notes to Myself

_____

_____

_____

_____

_____

_____

_____

_____

CHAPTER 5 FINANCIAL MANAGEMENT

Managing Your Finances

*"That money talks
I'll not deny.
I heard it once:
It said 'Goodbye.'"*

—Richard Armour

■ The Buck Stops Here

Among the many lessons you can learn in college, one of the most important may be managing your finances. Financial planning consists of more than merely managing and investing money. It includes making all the pieces of your financial life fit together.

One of the major reasons students cite for going to college is to improve their economic standard. Students believe that getting a college degree will make them more competitive in the job market (i.e., a high paying job), resulting in improved socio-economic conditions for themselves and their families. Potential income and status are further enhanced as additional degrees, particularly professional degrees, are earned.

College students are often on their own for the first time in their lives and are faced with the daunting task of managing their finances, developing and keeping a budget, and balancing a checkbook. Budgeting your financial resources is important in maintaining a reasonable standard of living. If you never have enough money, it can be quite frustrating. This is a good time to learn to develop a budget that shows your income and expenses so that you don't find yourself short of cash, in debt, and unable to pay your bills. You also need to develop a plan for financing your education so that you don't encounter unexpected financial problems which may cause you to withdraw from the university.

Many people with responsible jobs live paycheck to paycheck and rarely save any money. To avoid this situation, sound financial planning is advised. Why not start now? Learning to manage your finances is important so that when you graduate, you will already know how to budget properly and will be a step ahead of many other new professionals entering the work force.

■ Developing a Budget

The best place to start is preparing a budget plan which you can follow for a month. Exercise 1 will assist you in this process. Know how much money you have coming in from all sources (income) for a month, and be familiar with your fixed and anticipated expenses. Fixed expenses are items such as rent, your car payment, insurance, food, and gasoline for commuting to campus. Anticipated expenses include entertainment, new clothing, and purchases like a beeper or a cellular phone.

A good budget plan will include allocating some money to open a savings account or to invest. A "nest egg" could come in handy in an emergency situation when unexpected and unavoidable expenses arise. In these situations, you can use your savings to make payments instead of drawing from money needed for your ongoing monthly expenses.

A key item in developing a budget is accepting that you will have to monitor and probably reduce your spending. Monthly budgets that end in the "red" aren't allowed! If you don't want to decrease your level of spending, then you must find ways to increase your income.

Learning to manage your money and get more out of it is not only easy, it is fun as well. Items to consider in developing an understanding of your financial circumstances and financial management needs include knowledge of checking accounts and credit cards, paying bills on time, employment, savings and investments, and buying wisely.

■ Checking Accounts

Items to Consider When You Compare Banks:

- *Do they offer free checking?*

- *Are there monthly service fees?*

- *Do they cover your account when you overdraw, and if so, what fee do they charge?*

- *Do they offer an ATM card, and if so, is there a monthly service fee?*

- *If they provide an ATM card, are you charged a fee each time you use the card (not only at the bank that issued the card but at other ATM machines as well)?*

- *Do you have to maintain a monthly minimum balance, and if you don't, what is the penalty fee?*

- *What are the hidden fees the bank may charge for the "privilege" of having your business?*

Banks are as different as their names and have different ways of serving their customers. When you open a checking account, shop around for the best deal. Don't forget to check on the services offered at other financial institutions including credit unions and savings and loan organizations. Financial companies are very competitive and offer varying deals to attract customers.

Once you have selected a bank and opened a checking account, set up your checkbook. Be sure to keep your checkbook balanced by adding all deposits and subtracting expenses as you write checks. Don't wait until your monthly bank statement arrives to learn that your account balance has dwindled to little or nothing!

Does your bank cover overdrawn checks? Most banks do not unless you have savings to cover the amount in question. "Bounced checks" are likely to result in charges from both your bank and the business which accepted your check. The business may turn you over to a collection agency to recover their money if the amount of the check was large. Bouncing checks can also affect your credit rating. When you attempt to make a major purchase such as a car or house, or even apply for a credit card, a bad credit rating could result in you not getting approved.

Once your monthly bank statement arrives, be sure to reconcile your account to the proper balance. This means reviewing every item on the bank statement and matching it against every item in your checkbook. Even if you're a penny off, accept the challenge of locating the mistake and correcting it. You'll actually feel good about it once you're done, although the exercise may sometimes be frustrating and time consuming.

■ Credit Cards

Credit card debt is at the highest level it has ever been in this country. The average debt on major credit cards among consumers between the ages of 20 and 30 years old has nearly tripled since 1990. If you don't want to become part of that statistic, be wary of credit cards. College students are easy targets for companies that use promotional gimmicks to get you to apply for their cards.

Cards are easy to obtain and you get a "free" t-shirt or a coffee mug besides! Did you ever ask yourself why credit card companies are so anxious to have your business? The answer is simple: college students are more likely than many other segments of the population to use their credit cards. College students, you included, frequently have limited financial resources coupled with a strong consumer instinct. Students like to buy things. Without cash, the easiest way to make a purchase is with a credit card!

Items To Consider in Choosing a Credit Card:

■ *Shop around for the best deal, including the lowest interest charged. Some cards have an annual fee and some do not.*

■ *Why pay an annual fee if you don't have to? The credit card companies are competitive, and you can often negotiate better deals with banks or credit unions than those used in their advertisements.*

■ *Consider getting a credit card that is also an ATM or a debit card; your purchases will be automatically deducted from your checking or savings account. (Be sure to write these cash charges down and keep your balances current and accurate.)*

There are good and bad reasons for having credit cards. Two good reasons are that they are safer to carry than huge amounts of cash when making purchases, and they enable you to establish a credit history. On the flip side, however, credit cards are easy to use, and you may find that you've made too many purchases, resulting in large balances and heavy debt. Once your balances grow too large, meeting the minimum payments becomes difficult. At this point, many students begin working extra hours, cutting classes, and may even drop out of school or find they are dismissed because of poor grades.

A word to the wise: if you can't live without one, have one major credit card and pay off your balance each time you receive your bill. The average balance for a college student's credit card is $2,400! The interest rate on some cards is higher than the minimum payment. Some people find it impossible to pay off their balances because interest rates are so high. Remember that interest starts accumulating immediately for new purchases when you carry forward a previous balance. It is also important that you become familiar with the grace period that your credit card company allows for payments.

If you find that you are in credit card debt, discuss the situation with your financial institution and arrange payments that meet your budget. The company may not be pleased with this course of action, but they'd rather have some payment than none at all, and they certainly don't want you to file for bankruptcy.

Bankruptcy should be the last resort for anyone to take, particularly for a college student. In 1996, approximately one million people filed for personal bankruptcy in the United States. For the rest of your life, filing for bankruptcy could return to haunt you when you attempt to make major purchases or receive credit. Seek credit counseling before you take this drastic step!

If you believe that you absolutely need a credit card, go ahead and get one, but be honest with yourself about why you want that little piece of plastic. If you manage well with paying cash or writing checks for your purchases, stay away from credit cards for the present.

■ Pay Bills on Time

College students accumulate many types of bills, including credit card charges, college tuition and book costs, cellular phones and beepers, car loans, and if you live in an apartment instead of home, rent, utility, and phone payments. Be sure to include all of your monthly expenses in the budget that you develop.

Most monthly bills list the minimum payment due as well as the payment due date. If you miss the payment deadline, late charges are applied. You'll also be penalized if you don't make the minimum payment. Always try to pay the full balance of each bill or pay more than the minimum amount due (if you can't pay the balance). This will help you avoid those late charges or interest payments.

Key Items to Remember:

- *Pay bills on time!*

- *Pay the full balance if possible, and if not, pay the minimum amount due.*

- *If you have trouble making payments, discuss your situation with your financial institution.*

- *Seek credit counseling.*

Be aware that late payments may also affect your credit rating. Credit card companies and banks where you have loans often report consistent late payments or other payment problems to their credit agencies. This is why it is important to make payments on time or discuss your payment problems with your financial institution.

■ Increasing Your Income

There are various ways for you to increase your income to assist you in meeting ongoing expenses and avoiding debt. Foremost among the recommendations is a part-time job. Before you commit to a job, make sure that you weigh carefully the demands of working. Be sure it doesn't interfere with your real reason for being here: academics. Many students find it necessary to work in order to attend college. Successful students recognize that the emphasis must remain on attending classes and allowing adequate study time.

Many students find it more beneficial and enjoyable to work on campus rather than in the community. Various jobs are available throughout campus. These positions can be found through personal contacts or through postings in the university's Personnel Office, Financial Aid Office, or Career Services Office. Some students are eligible for College Work Study positions. These campus jobs are funded by both the Federal Government and the university and are awarded as a part of a financial aid award through the Financial Aid Office.

For positions off campus, students can use personal contacts, including family, family friends, and former employers, apply in person at various businesses, or visit the university's Career Services Office to peruse listings for part-time employment.

Remember that the purpose of working part-time is to earn money while you're getting an education. A part-time job should **never** interfere with your education.

Key Items to Remember:

- *Consider a part-time job to increase your income, but make sure your part-time job doesn't interfere with academics.*

- *Look for a part-time job on campus.*

- *Check your eligibility for the College Work Study Program in the Financial Aid Office.*

- *Apply for financial aid, scholarships, or grants to increase your income.*

- *If your finances permit, consider investments and other savings programs.*

Another way to increase your income is borrowing money; however, this raises your debt and requires repayment. A large purchase, a car for example, may require that you borrow money. The monthly payment for the loan must be added to your budget expenses.

Investments or interest on savings or other accounts represent an additional source of income. If your financial situation allows you to begin making personal investments in stocks, mutual funds, or long-term savings plans, be sure to get good advice and become an educated consumer. This will enable you to begin making sound investments now and hopefully receive a good return on your money for years to come.

Additional monies may also be available through financial aid, scholarships, or other grants, if you are eligible. Applications as well as information for various forms of aid and assistance are available in the Financial Aid Office. You can also check with the librarian at the Reference Desk in the Library who can direct you to more information regarding various scholarships and grants. Other forms of aid are available through scholarships awarded by community or social agencies. Information can be located through a Web search or Financial Aid. Be careful to read all eligibility and other documentation carefully and meet application deadlines.

■ Shop Wisely

Comparison shopping is another way to save your money. Wouldn't you visit several car dealerships if you were going to buy a new car so that you could get the best deal and save money? You should do the same with smaller purchases. Look for bargains and wait for sales. Some businesses will even negotiate the price of high-ticket items such as audio equipment, phones, and clothing because these items typically have a high price mark-up.

Sometimes it is better to pay a little more for a better quality item than to save some money on something that will not last as long. In the long run, you can save money by purchasing a better product because the cheaper item is more likely to require repairs or need replacement sooner.

It is a good practice to pay cash for your purchases. If you charge small items, you will probably make interest and finance payments if you don't pay the balance when you receive your bill. That means you will pay more for the charged merchandise. Keep the receipts for your purchases in case there is a question about your bill or you need to return them. Some stores will not allow exchanges or refunds without a receipt.

Another way to save on purchases is to use coupons or take advantage of store promotions. If you plan to make a major purchase, ask the store management when the item may go on sale. If you can wait until the sale, you will save money. When making large purchases, examine your budget first and determine whether or not you can afford the purchase. If the expenditure puts you in a situation where your expenses exceed your income, delay the purchase. You could even begin a small weekly or monthly savings plan to cover expenses associated with a large purchase.

■ Getting Out of Debt

You say that you've tried everything and you still can't get out of debt? There is always a solution! Here are a few recommendations frequently suggested by the "experts" on money and debt management:

- Use savings or cash to reduce or eliminate debt, but do not exhaust your entire savings in case you have a severe emergency and need immediate cash.
- Comparison shop for banks that offer better checking and ATM options and switch your account.
- Locate a better credit card deal and transfer your balances to the lower interest card.
- Cut up and discard the credit cards once the balances are transferred to the new card.
- Carry only one credit card and don't use it unless absolutely necessary!
- Seek credit counseling. Various resources are available in the community which offer advice on managing finances and debt.

Key Items to Remember:

- *Comparison shop, look for bargains, and negotiate.*
- *Pay cash for purchases.*
- *Keep receipts for purchases.*
- *Wait for sales.*
- *Use coupons and other promotions.*
- *Buy quality items.*

■ Check the Yellow Pages or contact the State Consumer Protection Agency or local Chamber of Commerce for consumer counseling recommendations. At the university, you can check with the Financial Aid Office or Counseling and Psychological Services for community referrals.

Filing for bankruptcy should be your last resort. Remember that this course of action remains a part of your credit history forever and may have a negative impact on your future financial transactions.

■ Summary

Most individuals work about 40 years in the course of their lifetime. At an annual average salary of $30,000, that means the "average" person will make more than $1,000,000 in his or her career. How will you spend all of that money?

Efficient and proper financial planning and management reduces stress and enables individuals to enjoy a better quality of life. Developing and following a budget, being knowledgeable about sound financial management, and learning and understanding the technicalities of finances can be invaluable for you in college and for the rest of your life.

■ Exercise 1. Monthly Budget

MONTH _____

INCOME

Source	Amount
1. _____	$ _____
2. _____	$ _____
3. _____	$ _____
4. _____	$ _____
5. _____	$ _____
TOTAL:	$ _____

FIXED EXPENSES

Type	Amount
1. _____	$ _____
2. _____	$ _____
3. _____	$ _____
4. _____	$ _____
5. _____	$ _____
6. _____	$ _____

ANTICIPATED EXPENSES:

7. _____	$ _____
8. _____	$ _____
9. _____	$ _____
10. _____	$ _____
TOTAL:	$ _____

TOTAL INCOME: $ _____

TOTAL EXPENSES: $ _____

Subtract expenses from income

BALANCE (Savings): $ _____   (Balance *must* be positive!)

■ Exercise 2. Developing a Budget

Your task in this exercise is to develop a budget for Sean, one of your classmates. This exercise can be done individually or in small groups. Each group should select a spokesperson to present the group's budget to the class. The time limit is twenty minutes.

The following are Sean's financial conditions for each month:

A place to live. He doesn't like roommates.

Three meals a day.

He has an old car that is paid for and gets 12 miles per gallon.

His car insurance is $80 per month.

He works 25 hours per week at $6.00 per hour. He gets paid every Friday. The Social Security deduction is 7.51%.

He has a school loan payment of $50 per month.

He likes to party.

He belongs to a health club. Dues are $50 per month.

He goes out to eat at least three times per week.

His girlfriend goes to school 500 miles away. He calls her twice a week.

His job is 10 miles from school. He lives midway between school and work.

His mom and dad give him money about every three months, usually $150 to $200.

He has two credit cards with a combined balance of $300.

He goes to a sporting event or a movie about once every two weeks.

CHAPTER 6 LEARNING STYLES
Learning with Style

T his chapter deals with learning styles and how the styles affect your learning. As you read through and do the exercises, keep in mind that there are no right or wrong answers. The goal is to help you find your learning style and use it to your advantage. In the process you will also find out more about your weaknesses. The more you know about yourself and the way you learn, the more effectively you can put that information to use in your college courses. Getting the most information from instructors and textbooks is important to your success. Discovering your learning style can help you be a better, more successful student (if you use the information).

■ What Is a Learning Style?

Before continuing, it is necessary to make clear just what is meant by learning style. Scholars have different opinions regarding what should or shouldn't be included in the definition. For our purposes, learning style is the characteristic and preferred way one takes in and interacts with information, and the way one responds to the learning environment. Think of your particular learning style as the way you prefer to learn new or difficult information, and the way you find it easiest and most comfortable to learn.

To illustrate, suppose that you are given a learning task. What is the first thing you would prefer to do to get the new information—read about it in a book; listen to someone talk about it; or do something with the information to prove that you know it? None of the ways is the right or best way, they are simply examples of different ways to learn. You may prefer one, or a combination of those listed. There is no best way to learn, just different ways. The goal for you is to find your preferred learning style.

Depending on which expert you ask, there are many different ways to consider learning styles and many ways to analyze them. This chapter will only touch on a few. If you feel that you would benefit from a more extensive diagnosis, you should get in touch with your campus counseling or testing center.

Your learning style may be more difficult to determine now than it would have been in elementary school. The reason is that as you get older and become a more mature learner, your learning style becomes more integrated. You have probably learned that you have to use many different ways to get information depending on the learning situation. When you answer the questions on the various learning style inventories given later in this chapter, keep in mind that you want to answer them thinking about your preferences. Answer them based on what you are most comfortable doing, and what's easiest for you. The more accurate the picture of your learning style, the more you can use it to help you.

■ Why Should You Know about Your Learning Style?

One of the goals of a college education is to make you an independent learner (also, a goal of study skills). There will be many things you will have to learn after you complete your degree, and helping you learn HOW to learn is an important aspect of your education. Knowing how you learn will help you begin to monitor your learning. The more aware you are of the way you learn, the better you can be at determining where you need help and where you don't.

As you study information by reading a textbook for example, if you are not understanding what you are reading, you need to make adjustments in the method you are using. You may try one of several options—reading the material aloud, silently reading it over again, asking someone from your class to explain it, or whatever might work. If you know what your learning style is, you will have a better idea about the one or two strategies more likely to work for you. This makes you more efficient (you don't have to try everything to find a strategy that works) and it makes you more effective because you can change strategies and understand the difficult material more clearly.

Some research indicates that grades are better, and the learner is more motivated when taught using the preferred learning style. The research also indicates a tendency in learners to retain the information better. Although you can't usually make choices about how your instructors will present information to you, you can choose how you will study on your own. This independent studying is the way you will be getting more of your information in college.

Strengths and Weaknesses

Knowing your learning style can also help you understand why certain types of information are easier or more difficult for you to learn. Being aware of weaknesses can help you be prepared for them. For example, if you know that you have trouble with numbers, then you know that your math class (necessary for meeting general education requirements) is going to be difficult for you. You can be better prepared by scheduling the class at a time when you are most alert, finding a tutor early on in the class, or scheduling it during a semester when you can devote the necessary time and effort to it. Your awareness of weak areas will help you be prepared for problems and prevent some, instead of being caught by surprise.

By knowing your strengths, you can overcome the problems and weaknesses. If you know the ways you are most comfortable learning, you can use those to help you learn difficult material. If you know, for example, that you need to read information to really understand it, then you know that you have to read the text chapter before you go to the lecture class. Hearing about something is not your preferred way to get information. You have to prepare yourself to be a better listener by reading first (using a strength).

As indicated earlier, as you mature, your learning style becomes more integrated. This does not mean that you don't have preferences. It only means that you have learned how to get information and use your weaker areas better. You will not always get information in your preferred style, so you must learn to use those styles which are less comfortable for you. Some students learn this easier and more quickly than others. By helping you see your style, you can also find the areas which need attention. The ultimate goal for a student is to use any learning style comfortably depending what's best for the situation. That may not be practical, but you need to be fairly competent getting and using information in several ways. This will help you with instructors who use only one method of getting information across, and will give you more options when faced with difficult material to learn. Most of us learn better when we use more than one modality to get it.

■ What Is Your Learning Style?

Modality Strength

The first survey is an informal look at whether you prefer the auditory, visual, or kinesthetic modes. Auditory learners like to learn by listening. Visual learners prefer reading or watching, and kinesthetic learners learn by doing (touching or manipulating) or using their hands in some way.

Answer the survey by checking those statements which are MOST like you, or are like you most of the time.

Brain Dominance

The next inventory will help you determine your brain dominance. The results of this inventory and what brain dominance means will be discussed later in the chapter. Answer the questions using the answer sheet given.

Information Style

The final inventory will help you determine your preferences for taking in information and the way you work with that information. Answer the questions according to the instructions given.

Results

Now that you have these results, you can begin to see the way you prefer to learn. The results of the surveys are informal, and if you think you could benefit from a more in-depth diagnosis, you should contact your campus counseling or testing center. They will have other tests which will give you more information.

■ How Can You Use Your Learning Style?

Going back to the checklist for your modality strengths, look at your preferences regarding auditory, visual, and kinesthetic. If you have a strong preference for one over the others, you probably have some idea that you learn better if you receive information in a particular way. You would prefer to work with or react to information in that same mode.

If you don't find that you have a strong preference for one learning style over the others, you may have found that you prefer to receive information one way, but you would rather react to it or work with it in another way. Or you may have found that you are well integrated in these areas, and show no strong preferences in receiving or reacting to information.

The following suggestions will be categorized according to the modality area. It's a good idea to read over all of the suggestions, keeping in mind your strengths and weaknesses. The type of material you are responsible for getting in different classes should also be considered when choosing a strategy to use. Generally, the more senses you can use, the better you learn and remember the information. Sometimes it will be helpful to concentrate on your strong areas especially with difficult material.

Suggestions for Auditory Strengths

General Hints

You will benefit from hearing information—audio tapes, your own voice, or lectures.
You may want to make tapes of reading assignments or class notes.
Pretend that you are teaching someone else the information and explain it out loud.
Reading aloud notes or text material will help you.

Lecture Hints

Use a cassette tape player for pre-testing by asking yourself questions, leaving a 2–3 second blank space, and then giving the answer.
Use a cassette player to record difficult material from your notes and then listen to the information as needed.
Orally test yourself by asking questions from your notes.
Read aloud any difficult material in your notes.
If you can't read aloud, try vocalizing the words quietly.

Textbook Hints

Read aloud summary statements, headings, and subheadings before you begin reading a chapter.

Restate key ideas to yourself as you read material. Keep a "conversation" going with your text as you read (agree or disagree with the author, or question key ideas).

For difficult material, restate in your own words what you have just read.

Read aloud, vocalize, or whisper passages that are difficult.

Read vocabulary words and their definitions before you begin reading.

After reading, quiz yourself (aloud) over the vocabulary.

Orally quiz yourself over selected main ideas.

Tape yourself reading difficult text sections, and then go back and listen to them.

Suggestions for Visual Strengths

General Hints

You will benefit from seeing information—either in print or from videos, charts, or overheads.

It will be easier for you to remember what you read than what you hear.

When given information orally, you should write it down or take some notes.

Lecture Hints

Read the text before attending lectures.

Take notes over lecture material.

For difficult or confusing material, use a mapping technique along with notes (mapping is drawing a diagram of the material read, using only the main ideas, then showing the relationship among the ideas with lines connecting them).

Use white space on your page as a guide when taking notes (skip lines between main ideas).

To learn material, stare off into space and remember what the written information looked like on your page.

Textbook Hints

Preview chapters by reading the headings, subheadings, and outlines before reading the chapter.

Watch for topic sentences. Reread them to help you stay with the material being read. Underline topic sentences.

Draw a diagram, jot down a list, use mapping, or make a chart to help you retain difficult material.

Underline key words and concepts as you read. Marking your text will be very helpful.

Suggestions for Kinesthetic Strengths

General Hints

You learn best by doing. The more involved you are with material, the easier it is for you to learn.

You should try to find practical applications for information. When you can, do projects and experiments using what you learn.

Write information down.

Moving your fingers along the lines as you read may help.

Lecture Hints

Take notes and go back over them, making special marks for important material or material you need to go over more.

For difficult or confusing material, answer practice questions in writing.

Write difficult information in the air with your finger.

Use your hand as a marker as you go through your notes.

Textbook Hints

Use your hand or finger as a guide as you read.

For difficult material, draw a chart or diagram to help you understand what you read.

Underline important words and concepts as you study.

Making and using study cards will help you learn difficult material.

Use 3 x 5 cards with a question on one side and the answer on the other. You can also put charts, lists, and diagrams on small cards to use for studying.

Use your finger to point out summary information, main points, and headings and subheadings as you read.

■ Brain Dominance

Research on the two brain hemispheres began in the 1950s with Dr. Roger Sperry. Dr. Sperry found that the two hemispheres (or halves) of the brain processed information differently, and both were equally important to the whole person. The functions of the hemispheres had previously been found to be different—with speech being a left brain function and spatial (visual) capability being in the right. It was not known until Dr. Sperry's research that the processing of information was different for each of the halves. The left brain is linear and processes in a sequential manner, while the right brain uses a global process.

It seems that schools and their curriculums favor the left hemisphere. In other words, we are given a major dose of left brain learning in school, and the right brain is neglected. Most of us probably learned that success in school depended to a great degree on choosing the proper hemisphere to process information. We didn't consciously make this choice, but we could figure out what would be required of us, and we would do that to be successful. This may have caused many students problems if they were unable to use the left brain easily, or if they couldn't determine what to do to be successful.

Research findings indicate that the learning of most information is better when both the right and left hemispheres are used. If your results from the inventory indicate that you do not have a dominance in the right or the left hemisphere, and that you are integrated, you are achieving the best for learning. You can use both sides of your brain equally well. You can choose one over the other when the situation calls for it.

If you have a strong tendency or preference for either the right or the left hemisphere, you may find yourself having trouble in various learning situations. As with your modalities, integration is the key to becoming a better learner. Use the list of characteristics on the following page to find areas where you can develop or polish your weak areas. Also, use them to help you with difficult material—use your strong areas to compensate for your weak areas. The more integrated you become, the more you are free to choose different ways to process information, depending on what's best for a given situation.

The box on brain dominance characteristics lists some of the characteristics of left brain dominant and right brain dominant people. You will find characteristics in both lists that describe you, but you should find more in the list that corresponds to your results on the survey. If you are an integrated person, you should find that the two lists have about an equal number of characteristics which fit you.

■ Information Style

In the final learning style inventory, you indicated your preferences for perceiving and processing information. Look at the descriptions on the following page. This will give you a clearer picture of your preferences.

These categories came about as the result of research done by Dr. David Kolb in the early 1970s. The survey that you took is the result of Bernice McCarthy's research of the 1970s. Many other researchers have come up with similar findings over the years. The researchers have been experts in the fields of psychology, education, and business. Their findings are amazingly close when defining characteristics of people in the four areas (although their names for the different styles are different).

Most of us can perceive information either abstractly or concretely and then process it actively or reflectively, but we are more comfortable perceiving and processing in a certain way.

Whether we perceive or process information one way or another is probably the result of heredity, past experiences, and the demands of the present environment on us. We would be better learners if we used each information style equally well, based on what the situation required. When you read over the descriptions of the information styles, think about ways you can build on your strengths and develop your weak areas.

The way you perceive and process information influences the career choices you make, the way you get along with others, the way you solve problems, and the types of subjects you prefer, to mention only a few. You will probably be more comfortable if you follow your natural inclinations. The problem may be that you have had to use one information style so much up to this point, that you have stifled your more natural choice. Again, integration is the key, and the more you can refine your skills in all areas, the better off you will be. You may make some discoveries about your true preferences along the way!

Now that you have some idea of your learning style, you may begin to see how difficult it is to separate the areas. You may have found that you had trouble with some of the questions because you could think of instances when all of the answers fit with your preferences. That's good, because it shows that you can use more than one learning style when faced with a situation calling for one over another.

Refining your skills in weak areas is important to help you become more integrated. The more integrated you are, the more flexible you can be in learning situations. You can use any number of skills and strategies which will help you. Knowing your strengths helps you when you are faced with a difficult learning task because you can use the strategies best suited for your learning style.

Brain Dominance Characteristics

Left Hemisphere	Right Hemisphere
Objective	Use visualization
Rational	Intuitive
Sequential and systematic	Rely on images for thinking and remembering
Like right and wrong answers	Risk-takers
Structured	Need neat environment
Questioning	Long-term memory good
Need constant reinforcement	Short-term memory bad
Contract-liking people	Prefer subjective tests
Organized	Random learning and thinking
List makers	Short attention spans
Time conscious	Respond to demonstrated instructions
Follow directions closely	Need touching
Rely on language in thinking and remembering	Don't read directions
Good planners	Don't pay attention
Accomplish things quickly	Pilers
See cause and effect	More flexible
Prone to stress-related ills	More fun loving
Perfectionists	Accident prone
Control feelings	Need to have goals set for them
Do one task at a time	Multi-tasks needed
Need gentle risking situations	Creative
Analytic	Visual learners
Solve problems by looking at the parts	Solve problems by looking at the whole picture
Verbal	Like humor
Recognize names	Recognize faces
More serious	Like improvising
Dislike improvising	Think geometrically
Abstract thinkers	Dreamers
Focus on reality	Assuming
Work on improving the known	Like fantasy
Like non-fiction	Inventors
Learn for personal achievement	Intrinsically motivated
Extrinsically motivated	Learn for personal awareness
Prefer objective tests	Free with feelings

■ What Other Factors Influence Learning?

In addition to your preferred learning styles, there are other factors which affect your learning. There are factors which affect your ability to study effectively and efficiently. Some of these will affect you more than others. Some may not be an issue for you at all, but you will find some you should consider when planning where, when, how and what to study.

Consider the answers to these questions regarding your preferences. Are writing assignments easier for you than oral ones? Would you rather write a paper or give a talk on a subject? (Tough choice!) Do you feel that you do a better job when you write or when you speak on a subject? Is it easier to get your thoughts down on paper or to talk about them? The answers to those questions will help you determine your preference for oral or written expressiveness. You will have to do some of both, but you can make course choices based on this knowledge.

Another option you may have in some of your classes is whether to participate in study groups. If you are the type of person who is comfortable in a group, then they will help you. Others, who learn better alone, may find a study group a liability. There are times when working with a group can help you understand material because the group can exchange ideas. Material may become clearer as you discuss it among the group members. Know your preferences and study accordingly.

Motivation plays a role in your learning. Are you learning for the pleasure of learning—to become more aware of the world around you, and to broaden your knowledge? Or are you learning with that one goal in mind—a degree? If the achievement of that goal is the only reason you are learning, you are approaching your education differently than the person who is learning to increase knowledge.

Being aware of your locus of control can help you understand your motivation. Locus of control is your perception of what accounts for the successes or failures in your life. It can be either external or internal. If external, then you attribute success or failure to outside forces (family, peers, fate, enemies). If internal, you attribute success or failure to the consequences of your own actions. You probably have a tendency toward one or the other, but do not see everything one way or the other. If this is a problem for you, you may need to work on changing your outlook.

Other factors which may influence your ability to learn or study are given in the following list.

> Noise level—from complete quiet to lots of noise
> Light—from low to bright
> Temperature—from warm to cool
> Time—early morning to late evening (the time you feel most alert)
> Position—sitting to lying down

Try to choose your ideal learning environment taking these factors into consideration. Consider others that impact you. Complete the sentences in the Environmental Factors Worksheet with your preferences for YOUR ideal study environment. Answer with the first thing you think of, and don't spend too much time thinking about them.

Analyze what you have just written. You may want to go back and revise, but you should not change answers unless the new one is definitely a stronger preference. Use the information to set up your study environment. Think about what you can change, and how you can adapt to those you cannot change.

What Are Teaching Styles?

Faculty members are learners from way back (and should still be learning). They also have learning style preferences. Those preferences had something to do with the choosing of their academic fields. The instructors also have teaching styles as a result of personality traits, learning preferences, goals, motivation for teaching, job satisfaction, and other factors.

Information Style Descriptions*

CONCRETE EXPERIENCE: *A high score in this area indicates a receptive, experience-based approach to learning where feeling-based judgments are most important. These individuals tend to be people oriented. Theoretical approaches don't hold much weight with them. They prefer to treat each situation as a unique case, and this is a problem with a theory. They learn best from specific examples and being involved. Individuals who emphasize concrete experience tend to be oriented more toward their peers and less toward authority figures in their approach to learning. They benefit most from feedback and discussion with fellow "concrete experience" learners.*

ABSTRACT CONCEPTUALIZATION: *A high score in this area indicates an analytical, conceptual approach to learning where logical thinking and rational evaluation are most important. These individuals tend to be oriented toward things and symbols and less toward other people. They prefer to learn in authority-directed, impersonal learning situations. They learn best when theory and systematic analysis are emphasized. They benefit little from unstructured learning approaches where discovery is important. They find these situations frustrating.*

ACTIVE EXPERIMENTATION: *A high score in this area indicates an active "doing" orientation to learning and processing information. These individuals learn best when they can engage in such things as projects, experiments, and homework. They will prefer small group discussions over passive learning situations such as lectures. They tend to be extroverted.*

REFLECTIVE OBSERVATION: *A high score in this area indicates a tentative, impartial, reflective approach to learning and processing information. These individuals make judgments based on careful observation. They prefer learning situations such as lectures where they are allowed to be impartial, objective observers in a learning situation. They tend to be introverted.*

You can also analyze your "Information Style" one step further by looking at the specific ways that you prefer to perceive or take in information and then the way that you prefer to process or do something with that information. Do this by determining which of the following is your strength: CE or AC _____ and RO or AE _____. This gives you a clearer picture of your preferences, and descriptions follow. You will want to look over each definition, but the one which describes your two strengths as suggested above will be most likely to best describe you.

ABSTRACTLY PERCEIVE (AC) & REFLECTIVELY PROCESS (RO): *Look for facts; need to know what the experts think; learn by thinking through ideas; prefer to learn by watching and thinking; more interested in ideas and concepts than people; like to collect data and critique information; thorough and industrious; will re-examine facts in perplexing situations; they enjoy traditional classrooms—schools are designed for them; function by adapting to the experts. Possible careers: basic sciences, math, research, planning.*

ABSTRACTLY PERCEIVE (AC) & ACTIVELY PROCESS (AE): *Need to know how things work; prefer to learn by testing theories in ways that seem sensible to them; learn by thinking and doing; need hands-on experiences; enjoy solving problems and resent being given the answers; have a limited tolerance for fuzzy ideas; need to know how things they are asked to do will help them in "real" life. Possible careers: engineering, physical sciences, nursing, technical areas.*

CONCRETELY PERCEIVE (CE) & ACTIVELY PROCESS (AE): *Need to know what can be done with things; prefer to learn by doing, sensing, and feeling; adaptable to change, and love it; love variety and situations calling for flexibility; tend to take risks; at ease with people, but sometimes seen as pushy; often reach accurate conclusions in the absence of logical reasoning. Possible careers: sales, marketing, action-oriented jobs, teaching.*

CONCRETELY PERCEIVE (CE) & REFLECTIVELY PROCESS (RO): *Look for personal meaning; need to be involved personally; learn by listening and sharing ideas; prefer to learn by sensing, feeling, watching; interested in people and culture; divergent thinkers who believe in their own experience; excel in viewing concrete situations from many perspectives; model themselves on those they respect; function through social interaction. Possible careers: counseling, personnel, humanities, organizational development.*

*Source: Concept & Ideas created by Bernice McCarthy and David Kolb.

When you are in a classroom setting where you feel comfortable and everything feels right, you are probably with a teacher whose learning style matches yours. When you are uncomfortable and feel out of place, the teacher may be someone whose learning style is different from yours. Since it isn't always possible to be matched up with a teacher who learns as you do, you must learn to adapt to the teaching style being used by each instructor. The more you can learn to use different styles, the more readily you can identify and adapt to teaching styles.

Many instructors have a tendency to teach the way they learn. You can make some guesses about their preferred learning styles by analyzing the predominant way material is presented and the atmosphere of the classroom. Material can be presented visually—videos, demonstrations, or diagrams on the board or overhead. It can be primarily an auditory presentation with lecture or audio tapes. Hands-on activities and experiments would be kinesthetic. You will find a combination in most classrooms, but look at the predominant one, or the one your instructor seems most comfortable using.

When you are in a classroom that is unlike your preferred style, you will have to work harder at concentrating and understanding. You may have to find extra materials to help you understand. It's imperative that you adapt to be successful.

A number of factors are used to describe teaching styles, and there are different ways of looking at and determining what constitutes a certain style. One area that will be important to you is the way an instructor communicates and interacts with students. At one extreme, there is the instructor who is formal and authoritative, and at the other extreme, the instructor who is very informal and casual. Most teachers fit in somewhere between the two extremes. If you find yourself not getting along with an instructor, think about this aspect and what you are most comfortable with, and you may have a clearer picture of the problem.

Again, you can't always be matched up with someone just like you, but you can ask around about specific teachers' styles. If you prefer a lecture setting, where students work independently and are expected to assume responsibility for learning, then find an instructor who is like that (especially for difficult classes).

However, if you are more comfortable in an informal setting where the instructor uses small and large group discussions and acts as a guide through the learning process, you will want to look for this kind of instructor for the more difficult classes.

You should be aware of teaching styles. You may find it helpful to analyze your teachers a little at the beginning of a class. You will then know whether you are going to feel comfortable in the class or need to adapt somewhat. The earlier you know this, the better your chances for success in the class.

■ Summary

Learning style has been defined as the way you perceive or take in information, the way you process that information, and the way you react to the learning environment. You were given inventories to determine your modality strengths, brain dominance, and information style. Knowing about your learning style is important to you because it can make you aware of your strengths and weaknesses. You can use this information to be a better learner by using your strengths to help you with difficult material. Your weak areas are where you need to develop or improve your skills to become more integrated. Being more integrated means being able to adapt to the best learning strategy for the learning situation.

Many factors influence your ability to learn and study. The more awareness you have of these and your preferences, the better you can set up your learning environment to be the most efficient and effective for you.

Teaching styles of instructors also influence your classroom experience. Being aware of the different teaching styles you may encounter will help you be prepared to adapt when necessary.

Complete the following with what you have found in this chapter.

MODALITY STRENGTH: Auditory   _____

Visual   _____

Kinesthetic   _____

BRAIN DOMINANCE: Left   _____

Right   _____

Integrated   _____

INFORMATION STYLE: Concrete Experience   _____

Abstract Conceptualization _____

Active Experimentation   _____

Reflective Observation   _____

(CE or AC) + (AE or RO)

_____   _____

LEARNING STYLE REFLECTIONS:

_____

_____

_____

_____

_____

◼ Modality Checklist

Check the statements below which are most like you, or like you most of the time.

1. ☐ My emotions can often be interpreted by my general body tone.
2. ☐ My emotions can often be interpreted by my facial expressions.
3. ☐ My emotions can often be interpreted by my voice (quality, volume, tone).
4. ☐ When I'm angry, I usually clench my fists, grasp something tightly, or storm off.
5. ☐ When I'm angry, I usually "blow-up" verbally and let others know I'm angry.
6. ☐ When I'm angry, I usually clam up and give others the silent treatment.
7. ☐ The things I remember best are the things I do.
8. ☐ The things I remember best are the things I hear.
9. ☐ The things I remember best are the things I read.
10. ☐ I remember what was done best, not names or faces.
11. ☐ If I have to learn something new, I like to learn about it by reading books and periodicals or seeing a video.
12. ☐ I like to learn through real experience.
13. ☐ I enjoy learning by listening to others.
14. ☐ I am easily distracted by sounds.
15. ☐ I am easily distracted. I have a short attention span.
16. ☐ I am easily distracted by visual stimuli.
17. ☐ I understand spoken directions better than written ones.
18. ☐ I remember what I have read better than what I have heard.
19. ☐ I like to learn most by building or making things.
20. ☐ I remember names, but forget faces.
21. ☐ I remember faces and forget names.
22. ☐ I tend to be quiet around others, and may become impatient when listening.
23. ☐ If I have to learn something new, I like to learn about it by having it told to me (lectures, speeches, tapes).
24. ☐ I enjoy learning by reading assignments and class notes.
25. ☐ To remember things, I need to write or copy them.
26. ☐ I generally gesture when speaking, and am not a great listener.
27. ☐ I really enjoy talking and listening with people.
28. ☐ When solving problems, I prefer to attack them physically, and often act impulsively.
29. ☐ When solving problems, I prefer to organize my thoughts by writing them down.
30. ☐ When solving problems, I like to talk the problem out and try solutions verbally.

Score by marking the numbers below that you checked. Add up the total number of statements checked in each category. You will find that one area probably had more statements checked than the others. This would be your modality strength. If you do not find one clear strength, you probably are well-integrated in these areas, and can use the modality which best fits the learning situation.

AUDITORY:	3	5	8	13	14	17	20	23	27	30	Total _____
VISUAL:	2	6	9	11	16	18	21	22	24	29	Total _____
KINESTHETIC:	1	4	7	10	12	15	19	25	26	28	Total _____

■ Brain Dominance

Check the statements below which are most like you, or are like you most of the time.

1. ☐ I prefer to have things explained to me.
2. ☐ I prefer that someone shows me things.
3. ☐ I don't have a preference for verbal instructions or demonstrations.
4. ☐ I prefer classes where things are planned so I know exactly what to do.
5. ☐ I prefer classes which are open with opportunities for change as I go along.
6. ☐ I prefer both classes where things are planned and open to changes.
7. ☐ I prefer classes where I listen to "experts."
8. ☐ I prefer classes where I try things.
9. ☐ I prefer classes where I listen and also try things.
10. ☐ I prefer to take multiple choice tests.
11. ☐ I prefer essay tests.
12. ☐ I don't have a preference for essay tests or multiple choice tests.
13. ☐ I don't like to play hunches or guess.
14. ☐ I like to play hunches or guess.
15. ☐ I sometimes make guesses and play hunches.
16. ☐ I decide what I think by looking at the facts.
17. ☐ I decide what I think based on my experiences.
18. ☐ I decide what I think based on facts and my experiences.
19. ☐ I respond better to people when they appeal to my logical, intellectual side.
20. ☐ I respond better to people when they appeal to my emotional, feeling side.
21. ☐ I respond equally well to people when they appeal to my intellectual side or emotional side.
22. ☐ I prefer to solve problems by reading and listening to the experts.
23. ☐ I prefer to solve problems by imagining and seeing things.
24. ☐ I prefer to solve problems by listening to experts and imagining things.
25. ☐ I am primarily intellectual.
26. ☐ I am primarily intuitive.
27. ☐ I am equally intellectual and intuitive.
28. ☐ When I remember or think about things, I prefer to think in words.
29. ☐ When I remember or think about things, I prefer to think in pictures and images.
30. ☐ When I remember or think about things, I sometimes prefer words and sometimes prefer pictures.

31. ☐ I am very good at explaining things in words.

32. ☐ I am very good at explaining things with my hand movements and actions.

33. ☐ I am very good at explaining with words and hand movements.

34. ☐ I am almost never absentminded.

35. ☐ I am frequently absentminded.

36. ☐ I am occasionally absentminded.

37. ☐ I am very good at recalling verbal materials (names, dates).

38. ☐ I am very good at recalling visual material.

39. ☐ I am equally good at recalling verbal and visual material.

40. ☐ It is more exciting to improve something.

41. ☐ It is more exciting to invent something.

42. ☐ It is equally exciting to improve something or invent something.

43. ☐ I would rather read realistic stories.

44. ☐ I would rather read fantasy stories.

45. ☐ I don't have a preference for reading realistic or fantasy stories.

Score by marking the numbers below that you checked. Add up the total number of statements in each category. You will probably find that one area had more checks than the others. If so, you have a tendency for that area (left, right, or integrated) to be your stronger learning preference. If you are more integrated than left or right dominant, then you can use either side of your brain. A more detailed description of brain dominance is given later in the chapter.

LEFT BRAIN: 1 4 7 10 13 16 19 22 25 28 31 34 37 40 43   Total _____

RIGHT BRAIN: 2 5 8 11 14 17 20 23 26 29 32 35 38 41 44   Total _____

INTEGRATED: 3 6 9 12 15 18 21 24 27 30 33 36 39 42 45   Total _____

Concepts & Ideas created by David Kolb, Paul Torrance, and Bernice McCarthy.

■ Information Style

This survey is to determine the way you deal with information best. There are no right or wrong answers—just your preferences. Mark the statements which best describe your preferences. Mark the ones most like you, or like you most of the time.

1. ☐ I am energetic and enthusiastic.
2. ☐ I am quiet and reserved.
3. ☐ I tend to reason things out.
4. ☐ I am responsible about things.
5. ☐ I prefer learning to be "here and now."
6. ☐ I like to consider things and reflect about them.
7. ☐ I tend to think about the future.
8. ☐ I like to see results from my work.
9. ☐ I prefer to learn by feeling.
10. ☐ I prefer to learn by watching.
11. ☐ I prefer to learn by thinking.
12. ☐ I prefer to learn by doing.
13. ☐ When learning, I trust my hunches and feelings.
14. ☐ When learning, I listen and watch carefully.
15. ☐ When learning, I rely on logical thinking.
16. ☐ When learning, I work hard to get things done.
17. ☐ I like concrete things that I can see and touch.
18. ☐ I like to observe.
19. ☐ I like ideas and theories.
20. ☐ I like to be active.
21. ☐ I accept people and situations as they are.
22. ☐ I am aware of what is going on around me.
23. ☐ I evaluate things before acting.
24. ☐ I enjoy taking risks.
25. ☐ When I learn I am open to new experiences.
26. ☐ When I learn I like to try things out.
27. ☐ When I learn I like to analyze and break things down into their parts.
28. ☐ When I learn I like to look at all sides of the issue.
29. ☐ I am an accepting person.
30. ☐ I am a reserved person.

31. ☐ I am a rational person.

32. ☐ I am a responsible person.

33. ☐ I am an active person.

34. ☐ I am an observing person.

35. ☐ I am a logical person.

36. ☐ I am an intuitive person.

Score by marking the numbers below that you checked. Add up the total number of statements in each category. You will probably find that one area had more checks than the others. A detailed description of what these areas mean is given later in this chapter.

CONCRETE EXPERIENCE: 1   5   9   13   17   21   25   29   33   Total _____

REFLECTIVE OBSERVATION: 2   6   10   14   18   22   26   30   34   Total _____

ABSTRACT CONCEPTUALIZATION: 3   7   11   15   19   23   27   31   35   Total _____

ACTIVE EXPERIMENTATION: 4   8   12   16   20   24   28   32   36   Total _____

■ Environmental Factors Worksheet

1. The best time for me to study is _____
   _____

2. The best place for me to study is _____
   _____

3. My favorite study position is _____
   _____

4. My preference for noise when studying is _____
   _____

5. My favorite temperature when studying is _____
   _____

6. My favorite light when studying is _____
   _____

7. My preferred class to study first is _____
   _____

8. I can study best when _____
   _____

9. I can't study when _____
   _____

10. List anything else that you know about your preferences for studying. _____
    _____
    _____
    _____
    _____

CHAPTER 7 TEST TAKING
Taking Tests with Confidence

Introduction

Oh, no! Not another test. Whose idea are tests anyway? Who needs them? I sure don't! Have you ever found yourself thinking these very thoughts? Most people do not like tests, but they are a necessary part of the learning process, and they do have a purpose. One reason instructors give tests is to motivate students to learn. If you knew that you were not going to be tested on the textbook or lecture materials, chances are you would not spend as much time reading, studying, or taking notes in class. In other words, you probably would not try as hard to learn, even though you are in college for that very purpose. Another reason for giving tests is that they help the instructor assess how much and how well you have learned the course content and its applications. Homework alone is not always a proper gauge of a student's knowledge. Instructors do not have any real way to know that you are the one who did the assignment or that you know and understand the material.

Taking tests gives both you and your instructor some feedback on what you have learned. It helps you to know what you need to review. It helps the instructor to know what material was confusing to the class, what topics may need to be repeated, or whether or not his/her style of delivery needs to be changed. Test results also help to determine the grade you will receive for the class. Test scores combined with your homework, projects, participation, and attendance indicate how well you achieved the course objectives. This total effort determines whether or not you are ready for the next course. In a very real sense, a test is—first and foremost—a learning device.

Properly preparing for tests and learning the skills and strategies presented in this chapter will make you test-wise, contribute to improved test scores, and help you become a more confident student. When you have learned how to develop good study habits, take good notes, and practice the strategies from this chapter, you will no longer have any reason to fear or hate taking tests.

Pretest

How test-wise are you? Check yourself on the following:

	Yes	No
1. I never miss class, especially when I know we will be reviewing a test.		
2. I get as much information about the test as I can. I ask questions about the test format and what it will cover.		
3. I study and review for tests throughout the semester so I don't have to cram.		
4. I have well written, understandable class notes to use when I study.		
5. I make up practice tests for myself.		
6. I get enough sleep the night before every test.		
7. I always survey tests before I take them.		
8. I plan and use my testing time wisely. I allow more time for the questions that are worth the most points. I skip questions I am unsure of and return to them later.		
9. When I don't know the answer to a test question, I know how to increase my odds of guessing correctly.		
10. I know how to get a better score on essay tests.		
11. I double check my test before turning it in to make sure I have followed the directions, finished all of the questions, and to see if my answers make sense.		
12. I always review tests when they are returned and correct my mistakes so I won't make them again.		

The above are things good test-takers do automatically. How many of them do you practice regularly? If you checked NO five or more times, your test scores may not be an accurate reflection of your ability, and you may really benefit from implementing the skills you will learn in this chapter.

■ Strategies That Promise Good Grades

The only way to ensure success is by thoroughly preparing for a test. Here are several important suggestions to help you.

Attend Class

This is crucial. Even though you may read the textbook, the instructor often explains the material. S/he may give examples that are not in the book, expand on the information already provided, present a different point of view, or provide your class with additional handouts and other materials. You need to be there! Anything covered in class may be included on the exam.

Class attendance also proves to the instructor that you are putting forth the effort to learn the material and that you want to earn a good grade. Often the class prior to the exam is used for review. The instructor usually will give you information to properly prepare for the test. This is the time for you to ask those questions that your classmates will be glad you asked.

Find Out about the Test

If you have certain facts about the test beforehand, you can plan your study strategies. What do you need to know about the test?

- ■ How long will the test be?
- ■ What type of test is it going to be?
- ■ What topics will be covered?
- ■ Will the questions be true/false, short answer, multiple choice, or essay?
- ■ Are the questions from the textbook, notes, or both?
- ■ Will there be extra credit questions?
- ■ Will the test be open-book?
- ■ How much will the test count toward the final grade?

Study Throughout the Semester

If you start studying from the first day and consistently review it, the material will stay in your mind. Cramming the night before a test opens the door for failure. The material is only in your short-term memory; therefore, you may not retain the information as readily or retrieve it as easily. Data may become confused, and you will become tense and tired from staying up all night.

- ■ *Study the most difficult concepts first.* You have a better chance of learning difficult material when you first begin to study, before you get tired.
- ■ *Review before you go to sleep.* Recent studies about brain function and memory show that your mind continues to work on problems during dream stages of sleep. Memory and problem solving ability improved with 6 or more hours of sleep. Each extra hour—up to 9 hours—of sleep provided significantly better results.
- ■ *Find a study partner or group.* You will learn better when you study together. It will force you to put your thoughts into words. In the exchange of notes, ideas, questions, and other materials, you will learn from each other. Helping others will help you on test day.

- *Don't just memorize;* try to understand the relationship between ideas, facts, and/or problems. You need to understand the material, and you need to be able to apply what you have learned.
- Whenever possible, *use study guides.* Your instructor may provide them for each class, they may be a library resource, or they may be purchased in the bookstore.
- *Read over your notes, homework, study guides, and quizzes* from the class. Don't forget to read the introductions, summary, glossaries, chapter review questions, chapter tests, and examples from the textbook.

Try to Predict Test Questions

One of the most effective test preparation techniques is to try and anticipate what will be on the test. Based on the textbook and lecture notes, try to predict the questions that your instructor might ask. Be sure to look over your notes for information that you've marked as important, and turn your chapter headings into questions. In math, make sure you practice every type of problem that was presented. If you do all of this, you will be prepared to take any test.

Note the Instructor's Style

Knowing what the instructor is looking for will help you know what to study. Usually s/he will be consistent with a particular type of test. Preparing for an objective test requires a different study technique than preparing for an essay exam. Talking with other students who have already taken the course can help you to know what to expect on the test.

■ T-Day (Test Day)

On the day prior to T-Day (test day) review previously read study materials just before you retire for the night. Get a full night's sleep so that you will be refreshed and able to think clearly during the test.

On test day be sure to set the alarm and get up on time. Eat a light, healthy breakfast. Wear comfortable clothes to the test, preferably layers so you can add or remove pieces if the room seems too warm or too cold. Exercise the same kind of common sense as when you study. Bring the proper supplies to class—whatever is needed for the test. If the test is open book, bring the textbook and your notes. If you need a dictionary, ruled paper, or a special pencil and/or eraser, be sure to include these in your backpack that day. Arrive a few minutes early in order to relax and get prepared to take the test.

Before taking the test, relax. When the test arrives, be sure to write your name on the paper. **Read all the directions carefully.** Immediately jot down key words before you forget them so that you can refer to them later. Preview the test and plan your time. How many questions are on the exam, and how many points are each of them worth? How much time can you allow for each question so that you complete the entire test? Also, allow a few minutes at the end of the exam to review your responses. Then answer the easy questions first and return to the difficult ones.

Write all answers clearly. If the instructor cannot read your writing, s/he may mark your answer wrong. Make sure that what you have written is a complete thought and grammatically correct. In math, be sure you have worked out all your problems to completion and that you used the correct equations. Always read word problems carefully; ask yourself what information you have been given and specifically what you are asked to solve. With all math problems, but most especially with word problems, check to see if your answer makes **common sense**!

Do not get anxious when other students finish the test and you are still working. Just because they finish does not mean that they have the correct answers. Before turning in your test, review the answers and check for mistakes, add information, fill in any missing blanks, and proofread your spelling and grammar. On math tests, check signs, exponents, decimals, zeroes, etc. Remember that changing your answers arbitrarily is not a good idea. If you studied sufficiently and attended class regularly, your first impression is often correct. You should never change answers unless you are certain the first one is wrong.

■ Kinds of Tests

Exams are of two basic types. You are either expected to *recall* what you have learned during the semester or to *recognize* the answers to the questions being asked. It is sometimes easier to respond to questions when the choices are given to you. That is why many students prefer multiple choice or true/false tests.

Recall Tests—Essay, short answers, and fill-in-the-blanks are tests given to measure how much you can recall. You have to supply the needed information in order to answer the questions.

Recognition Tests—Recognition tests seem to be the easiest type of tests for most students. All you have to do is be able to recognize the answer from the choices given. Multiple choice, matching, and true/false tests fit into this category.

You might prefer one type of test to the other, but chances are you will encounter both types of tests. It is helpful to use some good test-taking strategies to enhance your chances of success. Let's look at the various kinds of test questions and identify ways to do better on each.

■ Strategies to Improve Your Test Scores

Sentence Completion or Fill-in-the Blank Questions

Fill-in-the-blank and sentence-completion statements require you to supply missing information. Read the questions carefully and decide on your answer. Look for key words to help you determine the correct answer. If you have studied the vocabulary, these questions should not be difficult.

Look for clues. The verb form of the question will tell you whether the answer is singular or plural. The number of blanks may tell you how many words make up the answer. If "an" rather than "a" precedes the blank space, your answer will begin with a vowel or an "h" instead of a consonant. If you are not sure how to interpret a question/problem, ASK!

How would you fill in the following blanks?

1. In October, _____, the stock market "crashed" to begin the Great Depression.

2. An _____ person can be trusted.

3. The U.S. entered World War II in 1941 after _____ planes attacked
American Naval ships at _____ _____.

In the first item, you are asked to complete the date by adding the year (1929). The missing word in the second item is an adjective that begins with a vowel or a vowel sound. A logical choice would be the word honest. The third item asks for an adjective that describes planes (Japanese) and then a noun that names the location of the naval ships (Pearl Harbor).

Multiple-choice Questions

Many students and instructors prefer multiple-choice tests because they provide specific answers to each question. It is easier for the instructor to grade this type of test because students can put their answers on scantron sheets, and tests may be corrected electronically, or, the instructor may have an answer key that makes for speedier scoring. Many students prefer these kinds of tests because they have a chance of guessing correctly when they do not know the answer. However, if the instructor deducts points for wrong answers, it may not be advantageous to guess.

Multiple-choice questions consist of two parts. The **stem** is the statement, question or part that needs to be completed. Then, there are typically four or five **possible answers or choices**. One option will be correct; the others will be distracters.

■ Watch for key words. Underline them so they stand out and help you focus on the major points. As you read the question, try to answer it without looking at the options. Then read the choices to see if any match the answer you gave. Do not make a choice without reading all the responses! Eliminate the obvious distracters to improve your chances of choosing the correct answer.

■ Be on the lookout for statements with absolute words or extreme modifiers. They are almost always incorrect because they do not allow for an exception. Very few things in life are absolute.

Ex. Elderly patients experiencing dementia

a. are always diagnosed with Alzheimer's disease.
b. only lose their verbal skills.
c. are never able to reside in their own homes.
d. sometimes exhibit aggressive behaviors.

The only answer that does not contain an absolute word is "d."

■ Along with absolute words, be aware of statements such as "all but one" or except for one." This means the majority of the options are correct.

Ex. All but one of the following Americans landed safely on the moon.

a. Neil Armstrong
b. Edwin Aldrin, Jr.
c. Jackie Robinson
d. Michael Collins

In this case, the correct answer is "c." Jackie Robinson was a famous baseball player, but he never landed on the moon.

Absolute Words

All
Everyone
None
Always
Only
No
Invariable
Never
No one
Every

■ Be attentive to double negatives that can make a statement true rather than false.

Ex. In some states it is not illegal to

a. *transport heroin*
b. *manufacture LSD*
c. *use marijuana*
d. *sell cocaine*

The answer is "c." Not illegal means it is legal. Some states allow the use of marijuana for medical reasons.

■ If you can choose only one response, choose the one that provides the most complete answer.

Ex. During the Civil War, major Union victories were won at

a. *Shiloh*
b. *Gettysburg & Vicksburg*
c. *Bull Run*
d. *Gettysburg, Vicksburg, and Shiloh*

The correct answer is "d." Although "a," and "b," are true, "d" is more complete.

■ When two options are the same, you will know that neither is correct.

Ex. A polar bear can run up to

a. *1.5 miles per hour*
b. *5 miles per hour*
c. *15 miles per hour*
d. *1 1/2 miles per hour*

The correct answer will be selected between "b" and "c." "A" and "d" are the same.

■ When alternatives seem equally correct, select the one that is longest and contains the most information.

Ex. Down's Syndrome in infants is most often caused by

a. *Heredity*
b. *Smoking*
c. *Genetic and environmental factors*
d. *Alcohol*

■ When statements contain digits, the answer usually is not the extreme, but rather a middle number.

Ex. A pound is equal to

a. *1.6 oz.*
b. *6 oz.*
c. *16 oz.*
d. *66 oz.*

"A" and "d" are definitely out of the ballpark. The answer is "c." An exception to this rule occurs when the real answer is actually lower or higher than most people would expect.

■ When responses are similar, one is likely to be correct. When the choices are opposites, one of them is always wrong. The other is often, but not always, correct.

Ex. The Caribbean Islands are located in

a. The Pacific Ocean
b. The Atlantic Ocean
c. The Mediterranean Sea
d. The Panama Canal

In the above example, the Caribbean Islands are located in the Atlantic Ocean.

■ The correct answer should agree with the stem in number, gender, and person. It will also match grammatically.

■ Carefully read those test items that use two or three combined options as a possible response. Sometimes this is the correct answer. If you know for sure that more than one of the choices are correct, it is likely that "all of the above" are true. Be cautious, however, when you see "all of the above" or "none of the above." These could be trick questions, or the examiner may have used it only because s/he couldn't think of another choice.

■ Unless there is a penalty for wrong answers, if you cannot figure out the answer—GUESS. If you have studied, choose the answer that sounds right. If you guess randomly, choose "b" or "c." The odds are higher that the answer is one of the middle choices. *Go over your test when you are finished to make sure you have answered all of the questions.*

True/False Tests

Common Qualifiers

Many
Seldom
Almost
Sometimes
Frequently
Can
Most
Usually
Rarely
Ordinarily
Occasionally
Few
Some
Likely
Often
Possibly
Generally
Might

These are one of the most common types of examination questions. When answering, be careful not to overanalyze the questions. Do not be consumed with the fear that these are trick questions. Assume that the instructor is asking straightforward questions. Here are some things to watch for when answering true/false questions.

■ For a statement to be true, every part of it must be true. If any word or phrase is false, the statement is false.

Ex. Columbus tried to find a western route to the Orient in 1492 when he set sail with three ships, the Nina, the Pinta, and the Santa Clara.

The name of Columbus' third ship was the Santa Maria, not the Santa Clara.

■ Statements that have reasons in them are often false. Words such as "because," "therefore," "consequently," "the cause of," or "as a result of" are all words used to indicate reasons.

Ex. Obesity results from overeating.

This is a false statement because everyone who overeats is not obese. Likewise, obesity can be the result of a medical problem.

■ Statements that contain qualifiers leave open the chance for more "true" answers.

Ex. An instructor's personal preference generally determines which type of tests s/he gives.

This statement is true. Preferences often, but not always, influence tests.

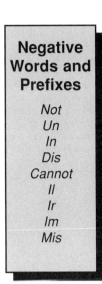

Negative Words and Prefixes

Not
Un
In
Dis
Cannot
Il
Ir
Im
Mis

- Some of the same rules that apply to multiple choice tests will also apply to true/false exams. Remember what we said about absolutes.

  Ex. All candy contains sugar.

  With so many substitutes today, sugarless candy is readily available. However, be careful, because some absolute statements can be true.

  Ex. Communication is always a two-way process.

- Watch out for negative statements. Your mind is more likely to "read over" negative words, causing you to miss them. If you are allowed to write on your test paper, underline negative words as you read to draw attention to them. In the English language, a double negative makes the statement positive. This is one of those grammar rules that you may ignore in conversations with your friends, but ignoring it on a test will cost you valuable points

  Ex. Different cultures must not be studied in an unbiased fashion.

  This statement is false. An easy way to avoid the double negative trap is to cross out both of the negatives and read the sentence without them. The above example would then read: *Different cultures must be studied in a biased fashion.* Reading the sentence this way makes it clear that this is a false statement.

- Once again, if you do not know the answer—GUESS.
  Do not leave unanswered questions on a test. If you've followed the above strategies and still don't know which answer to guess, mark the answer true. It is generally easier for instructors to write true statements when making up a test, as they usually want to accentuate the positive.

Matching Tests

Here are a few pointers for being able to logically match items on the test.

- Check to see if there are an exact number of matches. Also, check to see if any of the matches may be used more than once.
- Look for a pattern. Start with either column—whichever is easiest—and continue to work with that column.
- Read through the list of choices. Select the ones you know, and use them first to match with words in the other column.
- Use clues from other parts of the test.
- Apply all grammar rules—"a," "an," "subject/verb agreement," "singular/ plurals," etc.

Essay Tests

Essay questions require total recall, and they also require organization, grammar skills, and creativity. Most students either hate or love essay exams. There is no room for guessing on this type of test. You have to know the material, so you must be well prepared. You have an excellent opportunity to show what you have learned. Organization, grammar, spelling, and punctuation are very important on essay tests.

The key is to look for direction words and be sure to answer the questions accordingly. At the end of this chapter, there is a list of direction words with examples. By understanding what the instructor is asking, you can write a more effective response. Decide whether the question calls for fact, opinion, or both. Sometimes the instructor just wants facts; at other times the instructor wants you to form an intelligent opinion about a topic.

Here are some additional tips for answering essay questions.

- Jot down key words to help formulate your thoughts. A brief outline can help you ensure that your answer flows smoothly.
- Use the terminology from the course in developing your answer.
- Provide evidence to support your ideas. Be concise and to the point. Unnecessary repetition can lower your score.
- Some questions have multiple parts, so you need to address each part of the question, even if you only use one sentence to do so.
- Never leave ANY question unanswered unless there is a penalty for wrong answers. This could cost points that severely impact your grade.
- If you use dates, be certain they are correct. If you are unsure whether the year is 1876 or 1886, say "toward the end of the 19th century."
- Leave spaces between questions so you can make corrections or provide further explanations when you review later.
- Use the principles of writing from your English class. Be sure your answer has an introduction, body, and conclusion. You may use the question itself to introduce your response. Things to watch for include: correct spelling, subject/verb agreement, correct use of pronouns, logic, run-on sentences, sentence fragments, correct phrases, transitional words, etc.
- **Proof read all your work.**
- If you feel you are running out of time, outline the main points of your answer. The instructor will be able to see that you have some knowledge about the topic, and you may receive partial credit for your answer.

■ Direction Words

When writing an essay or short answer, your response should answer the question. Failure to follow the directions can drastically lower your grade. It is important that you understand the meaning of these common direction words so you can state your answer correctly.

Direction	Definition
Analyze	To break or separate the whole into its parts. To determine the nature, function, qualities, characteristics, relationships, and effects of the parts to the whole. In English, you may do this with a sentence; in science, with a substance; in math, with an equation. *Ex. Analyze the properties of water.*
Argue or Defend	To give reasons for or against something. A discussion or debate that supports or refutes a position. In preparing an argument, you try to defend a point or persuade others to a cause. *Ex. Argue whether or not courtroom proceedings should be televised.*
Comment	To present a pro or con opinion or viewpoint on a subject. *Ex. Comment on the choice of Beijing as a Winter Olympics site.*
Compare	To identify similarities and differences on a given topic. *Ex. Compare "Buddhism" with "Hinduism."*
Contrast	To stress the differences or dissimilarities among things; to show how things are "unlike" one another. *Ex. Contrast "assertive" and "aggressive" communication styles.*
Critique or Evaluate	To express your own views or the views of an "expert." You need to include positive and negative points/opinions. *Ex. Critique* The Raven *by Edgar Allan Poe.*
Define or Identify	To provide a clear and concise meaning, a comprehensive description, or the identifying characteristics. Do not use the term to define itself. *Ex. Define the term Existentialism. / Identify the major stressors for college students.*
Describe, Discuss, Explain, or State	Give a detailed account or picture, frequently in narrative form, to make something understandable. Include positive and negative points or cause and effect relationships for clarification. *Ex. Describe a balanced lifestyle. / Explain personality development from a Psychodynamic perspective.*
Diagram or Illustrate	To use a sketch, chart, graph, outline, labels, or examples to explain and clarify a point. *Ex. Diagram the anatomy of a heart. / Illustrate the human body's nervous system.*
Justify	Demonstrate or prove what is right, just, or valid by providing reasons or evidence for a decision or act. *Ex. Justify the use of pesticides in twenty-first century orchards.*
Label	To classify, designate, identify, and attach a name to some specific group or theory. *Ex Label the primary classes in the animal kingdom.*
List or enumerate	To provide an itemized list or to make points one by one in order. *Ex. List the qualities of a good public speaker. / Enumerate the steps involved in good decision-making.*
Narrate	To provide an accounting of something or to tell a series of events in story form. *Ex. Narrate the events that led to the economic blockade of Cuba.*
Outline	To summarize the main points or provide an organized listing of the main topics. *Ex. Outline the main events that led to the Civil Rights Movement.*
Paraphrase	To express an idea in your own words. *Ex. Paraphrase John Gardner's* Theory of Multiple Intelligences.
Prove	To present factual evidence and give logical reasons to support something. Frequently used in the sciences (tests or experiments) to establish something as true or valid. *Ex. Prove that Uranium 235 degrades to lead. Include all 17 steps.*
Relate	To show how things are connected with each other, to give cause and effect, or to explore relationships and correlations. This is usually done in narrative form. *Ex. Relate the importance of values, interests, and personality on career choice.*
Review or Summarize	To discuss the main points in a clear and concise manner. You may be required to give a critical analysis, as in a review of a book or play. *Ex. Review the study systems discussed in class. Summarize effective listening techniques.*
Trace	To narrate the development or process of something in a historical fashion, showing the sequence of events through time. *Ex. Trace the events that led to the exploration of Mars in the latter half of the twentieth century.*

■ Special Testing Situations

Open-book Tests

Many students feel that these are the easiest tests to take, but do not be led astray. Open-book tests are probably more difficult. They may have to be completed in a certain amount of time. Not only must you study and know where to find the material quickly for your answers, you must also learn to think critically. Questions are never verbatim. Always practice making up and answering test questions that you think the instructor might choose.

Take-home Tests

Every student's dream! But, once again, don't be misled. Take-home tests are usually more difficult and ask for lengthier answers. You will still need to study and know the material. The biggest danger is waiting too long before preparing for the test. You do not want to wait until it is in your hand before learning the material. Critical thinking is also an integral part of take-home tests.

Standardized Tests

Tests such as the ACT, SAT, COMPASS, and ASVAB are standardized tests. They are prepared by a testing service and administered under prescribed conditions. Although there are often different versions of the tests, the questions test the same content and require the same kinds of knowledge. Many times these tests are mandatory entrance or placement tests at colleges and universities, or they may be required for scholarships or enlisting in the military. There are several things to remember about standardized testing.

- *Prepare* sufficiently in *advance* for these tests.
- *Use study guides*. These resources are available in most libraries and bookstores. Preparatory classes may also be available in your area. These may be expensive; however, they will provide you with review and practice for the tests.
- Before taking the test, always *check to see if you will be penalized for guessing*. On the SAT test, a percentage is deducted for incorrect answers to discourage guessing.

Math Tests

Use all of the strategies that you use for other tests when taking math tests. Note the following special considerations:

- Break down complex problems, and work the steps one at a time.
- Show all your work in an organized fashion.
- Draw pictures or diagrams to help you visualize problems.
- Check your computations. Be sure you are using the right formulas, have the correct order of functions, and sined numbers are correct.
- Ask yourself if your answer makes common sense!

■ Test Results

What do you do when the tests are returned to you? This is a great opportunity to learn from your mistakes and to help you prepare for the next exam. Go over all the errors that you made. If the instructor wants the tests returned, jot down the kinds of mistakes you made in order to develop new and better strategies for the next test. Analyze the instructor's style of testing. Was the test objective or subjective? Were the questions taken directly from the book, from lecture notes, or from both? Was there a pattern in the answers that would help you guess in the future? What kind of mistakes did you make?

Never throw away a returned test until after the final exam. You may use these tests to review for that final and improve your grades. See if you need to further develop any of the following:

- More effective time management for studying and taking tests
- Better note taking techniques
- Reviewing throughout the semester
- Better study and test-taking strategies
- Reading and following directions accurately
- Providing more details for your answers
- Getting a full night's rest before the exam
- Eating a healthy breakfast the day of a test

■ Summary

Good test results require extra effort. Proper preparation for test taking includes class attendance, effective use of your textbook and notes, good study habits, getting information about the test beforehand, and practicing test taking. These are important components for good grades. If you learn to use the strategies suggested in this chapter you can improve your scores on exams and in your classes.

You can also learn from your mistakes by reviewing the test after it has been graded. In the future, do not repeat your errors. Set goals for improving your skills.

Name: _____ Date: _____

■ Journal Assignment

What exams do you have scheduled in the next few weeks? How will you use the strategies you have learned in this chapter on your next tests?

Think about several recent tests you have taken. Using the techniques you have learned from this chapter, how could you have improved your grade?

◼ Homework Activity

Examining Your Test-Taking Errors:

Review a test you have taken recently, on which you did not receive a satisfactory grade. Make a list of the reasons you did not do well on this test. Consider the quantity and quality of your preparation. Examine your errors. What went wrong? Write down everything you can remember.

_____

_____

_____

_____

_____

_____

_____

_____

_____

_____

_____

_____

_____

_____

_____

_____

_____

_____

_____

_____

Review a previous test on which you earned a good grade. List all of the reasons you did well on that test. What did you do right?

_____

_____

_____

_____

_____

_____

_____

Now think about an upcoming test in one of your classes. What grade would you like to earn? How much studying will it take to earn your desired grade? What exactly do you need to study to prepare properly for this test? List the things you will do to ensure that you get a good grade. Be specific about how, when, what, and where you will study.

_____

_____

_____

_____

_____

_____

_____

_____

_____

_____

_____

CHAPTER 8 MOTIVATIONAL LEADERSHIP

Motivate Your Way to Success

Welcome to College!

You have a lot of neat experiences ahead of you, some frustrating, and hopefully many rewarding. Are you excited about this new learning venture? Think back to your first day of elementary school. Do you remember how excited you were? Do you have that same enthusiasm today?

Unfortunately, many students associate learning with "school" and they don't have a lot of positive feelings toward school. Learning performance tends to drop as we go along in our academic pursuits. School is associated with "drudgery," and before we know it our attitude starts to be indifferent.

From *Practical Approaches for Building Study Skills and Vocabulary*, Second Edition by Funk et al. © 1996 by Kendall/Hunt Publishing Company.

Let's try and start fresh with a good attitude like we had in first grade!

Why Are You Here?

This is an important question for you to answer. There are several reasons why students attend college. Fill out the exercise titled: Why Are You Here?

You need to stop and think about why you are in college. Are your reasons for being here due to others? Will these people be responsible for your success in life? Will they be attending class for you? Taking your tests? Receiving your diploma?

A recent study at a midwestern university revealed the top three reasons chosen for attending college were:

1. To increase the chances for a higher paying career
2. To expand knowledge
3. To help ensure success in life

This is a good time to examine your values and decide what you feel is important. Fill out the worksheet on clarifying your values. These values affect the choices you make in life.

The Coat of Arms Exercise will help you think about your personal feelings. Fill in this worksheet and think about the priorities in your life.

The student who is "educated" is the one who has learned how to learn. It is important to be aware of your values and goals because that will help motivate you to do your best. You need to recognize what is important to you, and strive to reach your potential. A college education can help you develop a flexible and open mind, sharpen your ability, and enrich your life.

What Is a Successful College Student?

We all want to be successful. There is not one college student that attends college to be unsuccessful. How can we be successful? There have been numerous studies done in this area. Most of these studies show that successful students tend to possess the following characteristics:

1. *They have a definite reason for attending college.*

   You must decide what *you* want out of college. After completing the Exercise, Why Are You Here, you have had the opportunity to think about what is important to you.

2. *They have selected a vocation and are pursuing this course.*

   Don't panic if you don't have a career chosen. But, be aware that it provides motivation to have a career goal. Spend this first year trying out several courses in varying fields. Maybe one will ring a bell! When you have chosen your career, you will be motivated by a clearer sense of direction.

3. *They realize the need for understanding the material in each class and envision the value of it.*

A successful student does not study just to pass a test. They usually have a three-pronged approach to the material.

a. They master the basic facts. Without doing this, there is nothing on which to build.

b. They take these basic facts and draw supporting details in for a total picture.

c. They learn to "think" with the subject. Once you are able to explain a concept in your own words—it's yours!

This approach allows them to "learn" the subject matter, not just memorize it.

4. *They have a desire for success.*

The more success you experience, the more you will want.

"Success Breeds Success"

"Success Creates Interest"

What a wonderful feeling accomplishment can bring! Have you ever failed a class that you really liked? Probably not. Success can create interest, which further ensures success. One way we have of achieving success is the attainment of goals. Much more about that later!

5. *They have the will to succeed.*

Abraham Lincoln loved to read. It was told that he walked 20 miles to borrow a book. Would you exert that much effort? If we can't park close to the library, we probably will not bother to check out a book!

How can we develop this kind of will to succeed?

GOALS ⟶ SUCCESS ⟶ STRENGTHENS WILL ⟶ MORE SUCCESS

We can develop this will to succeed by the attainment of short-term goals. Small successes strengthen our will, and the strengthened will provides us with additional power to work even harder.

6. *They have developed good study skills.*

The definition of study skills is the efficient use of our mind and our time. The key word is "efficient." There are other phases of our life that need attention, and we need to develop study skills so we can accomplish the maximum in the minimum amount of time. Study skills are not instinctive, but something that we need to learn. The goal of study skills is independent learning. As long as you look to someone else for interpretation, you are not a free person intellectually.

7. *They know they must set priorities. "This is the time to learn."*

Rank your needs at this time. It is not necessary for school to be number one, but it must be extremely high on the list.

Consider this scenario:

Greg was studying for a physics test. Doug and Jeff were on their way for pizza and a movie. They stopped by Greg's room and invited him along. Greg's decision could be crucial toward a high grade on his test the next day. What would you do?

■ What Is Motivation?

Webster's Dictionary defines motivation as the condition of being motivated; an incentive or drive. How do we apply this to ourselves? Let's think for a moment about ourselves.

How many brain cells do you have?

Hint: A lot more than you think!

You have 13 billion brain cells. Do you feel smarter already? One thing you should be thinking about right now is how to use these 13 billion cells to their fullest potential. In this book you will be able to find several effective ways to learn; ways that are the best for *you*.

Let's imagine that we have an assembled computer sitting in front of us. This computer contains one million parts.

What is the first thing we would need to do in order to use it?

Hint: Think electricity.

O.K., we should plug it in to the electrical outlet. What do we need to make *our* 13 billion part computer work? Our electric current is called *motivation*. Motivation is what makes learning come alive!

What Is Your Source of Motivation?

Our source of motivation is human needs. The psychologist Abraham Maslow believed that all human beings have a need to grow, to develop abilities, to be recognized, and to achieve. He viewed human needs in hierarchical order. Some needs take precedence over others. We need to satisfy the lower needs in order to achieve the higher ones (see Figure 1). If we don't take care of our fundamental needs which are our basic physiological needs (hunger, thirst, sex) and our need to feel safe, then we have difficulty proceeding to the next level which involves our psychological needs. These in turn need to be fulfilled in order to reach the top which is our self-actualization needs. For self-actualized persons, problems become a means for growth. Wouldn't it be nice to view problems in this manner?

What Is the Difference between External and Internal Motivation?

1. *Internal Motivation*—These are motivational elements that are within ourselves. We have feelings of pleasure or disgust as we meet or fail to meet our own standards. This is the reinforcement level we should all strive to meet. We should try to find value in our work, enjoy success, develop an appropriate value system, and thereby reinforce ourselves for our efforts. People differ in what they think provides reinforcement.

2. *External Motivation*—These are motivational elements that come from outside stimuli. Rewards in the form of material things, privileges, recognition, trophies, praise, or friendship. These are a "public" way of saying a job is well done.

Critical Thinking

Todd felt he had prepared for his first major exam in geology. Science was difficult for him. He had attended all lectures, revised his notes, and read the chapters. He made an appointment with his professor to clarify some points that he didn't understand. He felt he was ready for the exam. When Dr. Jones returned the test, Todd had scored 94%. The reward of the high score was a real high! He felt successful, and knew he could continue to do well in this course. He called his parents that night and they were elated. Their praise echoed their feelings. Todd had received internal and external praise. Do you believe the external or the internal motivation that he received from the test score was the best motivator?

As you progress through school, internal motivators should become stronger. We should not always feel the need for external motivation. This doesn't mean we don't want external rewards, but its value should begin to lessen.

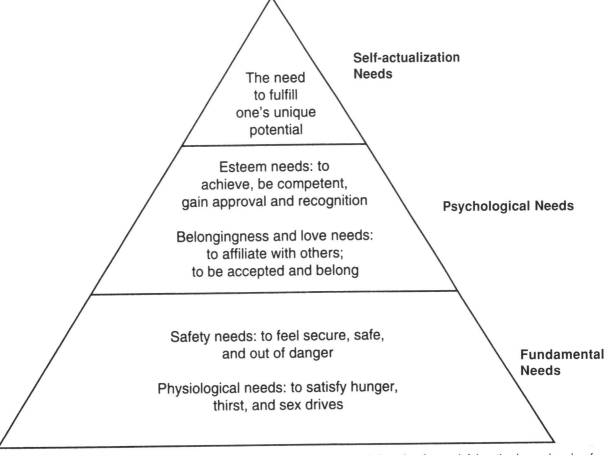

Figure 1 ■ Maslow's hierarchy of human needs. According to Maslow, it is only after satisfying the lower levels of need that a person is free to progress to the ultimate need of self-actualization.

■ What Are Your Goals?

Motivation is the first step in all goals. A goal should be something that you desire and that you will be motivated enough to try and reach.

Goals can be divided into three categories:

1. *Personal*—These will be determined by your value system. You have already filled out the Value exercise. This should give you an idea of what you feel is important to you. Personal goals can also include personal fitness, developing a positive attitude, and overcoming a bad habit.

2. *Academic*—You can be successful if you set your goals on what *you* want to get out of college. The exercise on reasons to attend college should also include some academic goals.

3. *Work Related*—What do you want from your chosen field of work? Improving your performance? Changing jobs? Learning new skills?

Why Do You Need Short-term and Long-term Goals?

It is necessary to have short-term and long-term goals. It is easy to lose motivation with only long-term goals. Short-term goals are necessary to act as our motivational elements. The accomplishment of these goals give us the will to succeed. Long-term goals clarify our direction.

What Are Some Important Characteristics of Goals?

There are four characteristics of goals that we will discuss. While you are reading about these characteristics, think about how you can apply these points to your life.

1. *Goals should be realistic*—A realistic goal is one you can reasonably expect to achieve given your abilities. If your goal is too high and you don't reach it, it can certainly affect your self-concept. If your goal is too low, when you attain this goal there is no real feeling of success.

   Amy attained a 3.0 (out of a 4.0) in high school. Her college goal was to attain a 3.0 average. Is this a realistic goal? Is Amy setting herself up for failure, or is this a possible goal?

   Bill was valedictorian of his graduating class. His goal in college was to maintain a C average. His goal was not high enough to give him the sense of accomplishment that he would need to make him feel successful.

2. *Goals should be measurable*—A measurable goal establishes a time frame and it also has a foreseeable outcome. You should have daily and weekly goals. Attaining these short-term goals will give you the successful feeling that you need to experience to keep you going. Semester, yearly, and other long-term goals (college degree, marriage, family) are also vital because they clarify your direction.

3. *Goals should be flexible*—Decide what you want to do and be willing to change your plans if necessary. Rarely do we set goals and follow through to completion without any problems. You might change your major, withdraw from a class, or experience any number of setbacks. Reassess your plan for reaching your goal. You might

---

Critical Thinking

Your long-term goal is to be a lawyer. Is that enough to motivate you to attend and be excited about the basic psychology class that you have at 8:00 a.m. on Monday, Wednesday, and Friday? Maybe at first, but as the semester rolls along there will be mornings that being a lawyer doesn't quite have the zip that it once did. The short-term goal of making a B in psychology that will complete three hours of general education requirements just might! (Hopefully your short-term goal will be to learn as much as you can about human behavior so you can effectively deal with people in your law practice.) It will help you to have a goal that you can accomplish in a short period of time to serve as an inspiration. An even better short-term goal would be to make a B on the first exam. Once this is accomplished, hopefully the adrenaline will flow!

---

need to revise it or make a new plan. It's alright to change your goals if you make a mistake or decide to change your plans.

4. *Goals should be specific*—The purpose of goals is to make us "act." In order for a goal to activate us, we must have specific objectives in mind. If we are too vague, we never receive the satisfaction of success that we should feel when we attain the goal.

Nancy's goal this semester is to attain a 3.0 grade point average. Peggy's goal this semester is to "do well" in her classes. Who will receive the greater satisfaction if they attain their goal? Who will know if their goal is met?

Goals do not have to be major events. Your goal for today may include:

Pick up cleaning
Read Chapter 3 in sociology
Do math problems 2.1 through 2.6
Clean the bathroom

These are specific goals. You will know at the end of the day if you have attained them. These are much more motivating than:

Run errands
Study
Catch up on housework

■ Is There a Relationship between Setting Goals and Academic Success?

After what we have learned to recognize about goals, this is an easy question to answer— Yes—Yes—Yes. Goals are activators, they provide a successful background that enables you to continue to strive. They are like gas to a car, food to our bodies, and rain to the grass.

The attainment of goals is also related to a positive attitude and high self-esteem. When we attain goals, we feel successful!

■ How Can You Develop a Positive Attitude?

Visualize yourself being successful. Jeni Burnett, a Pittsburgh State University basketball player, relates her success technique at the free throw line:

> *First of all, I block out the crowd noise. I dribble a couple of times and feel the ball. During this time I visualize my entire body. I think about my legs bent properly, my arms' and hands' position, my release, the ball being "up," the correct spin, the right arch, my follow-through. I see the ball "swish" the net.*

It is amazing how powerful positive thinking can be! It is also very contagious. Of course, negative thinking is also contagious. It is unbelievable how a "down" person can pull others "down" with them. We all know some people that constantly dwell on the negative side of life. They sometimes do not even realize it—it has become a way of life.

> *Fred woke up with a headache. He had worked a double shift the previous day. His roommate, Jim, was on his way out the door to class. Jim had actually read his history chapter and he hoped it would help him take better notes. Fred noticed it was raining; he had worked a double shift the previous day. He rolled over and muttered that he wasn't going to fight the rain to listen to Dr. Smith's boring biology lecture. It was annoying enough that he had a headache. He could have gotten the notes from Sue, but he recalled after his remark about her sweater that she probably wouldn't share her notes. He told Jim that he couldn't understand why teachers always seem to enjoy frustrating students. There had to be more to life. Jim walked out the door to go to class. He was beginning to wonder why he got out of bed today.*

■ What about That Negative Voice?

Should we look at the negative side of a situation? We don't like to because being a "positive" person is crucial to our success. We also need to be realistic (unfortunately or fortunately—life is "real"). What are you going to do if you fail the first test in one of your classes? That is a possibility (distant, of course). What will your plan be? Inside we have two voices that are always screaming to get out of us. One is a positive voice, the other is the dreaded negative voice. Unfortunately, the voice seems to have more volume at the most inopportune times.

> *Jane came to college from a large high school. She took college prep classes and maintained a B average. She was active in a lot of social activities in her high school. Studying was a concern, but certainly not a major one. She kept up in her classes with very little effort. Jane came to college and since she had experienced success in high school with very little effort, why should this change? The social scene was important to her in college (that's o.k.) and she knew everything would just fall in place. In sociology and biology her first exams fell on the same day. (Don't teachers ever get together and try to avoid this?) The night before the tests (as in high school), Jane sat down and started digging. "Surely, I won't need to know all of this, so I'll concentrate on my notes," she rationalized. "The notes are obviously what the teachers will think is important. After all, that is what they talked about!" A lot of the information didn't seem that vital, so Jane picked*

out what she thought would be on the tests. About midnight, after telling at least twelve of her friends how hard she was studying, she was ready to call it a night. After all, her biology test was at 11:00 and her sociology was at 1:00. There was a mild panic at 9:30 the next morning when she realized she had slept through her alarm. But, not to worry, she had plenty of time to shower and review once more. Food could wait until lunch.

The biology test was given to the class. How could it be that many pages? Where did he come up with these questions? She found a lot of questions that she thought she knew, but the wording was ridiculous! What a relief when that was finished! On for a quick lunch and the sociology test.

She thought, "These teachers must get together and decide to ask weird questions." She wondered if there was an upper level education class for teachers that taught them to ask sneaky questions. "Why don't they ask questions that come directly from the book? After all, they wanted us to read it."—were two thoughts that Jane had. Jane definitely needed a nap after these two tests. She wasn't very concerned until the tests were handed back. There must be a mistake! She had never made a D in her life! How could she have made a D on both exams? She quickly folded back the corner of the tests so no one could see. What voices were screaming to be heard?

This could and might very well happen to you. It's not important that it happened, but it's how you are going to react that is important. You can turn this experience into a productive event. Before you throw this book in the trash, let's analyze the situation. Which voices will be dominant?

"I'm not smart enough to be here!"
"The teacher is a jerk—he didn't cover this!"
"He tried to trick us!"
"I hate this class!"
"At least I did better than Sally."
"I didn't really understand, I just memorized."
"I could have used the book to help me understand the notes."
"Now I know the type of questions that he asks."

High school students are usually concerned with the "literal" meaning of their textbooks. This means they are interested in the exact meaning—the words that are obviously stated. In college it is important to have an understanding of the material so you can *apply* the information. Concepts or ideas should be the result of studying your text. Maybe this means one of our *goals* should be the understanding of what the author is trying to say along with your teacher's interpretation. What do you think?

■ Summary

It is important to think about *why* you are attending college. You should recognize your values and goals because they clarify your direction. Your motivation is directly related to achieving your goals. Success in our endeavors strengthens our will to succeed.

A good positive attitude is vital in achieving success in college as well as in life!

■ Exercise 1. Why Are You Here?

What are your reasons for attending college? Listed below are some reasons why some students attend college. Check those which are closest to the reasons why you are here.

_____	1. I want to earn a degree.
_____	2. My friends are in college and I want to be with them.
_____	3. I want to please my parents.
_____	4. I want to meet new people.
_____	5. I want to prepare myself for a career.
_____	6. College graduates make more money.
_____	7. I want to broaden my knowledge.
_____	8. College graduates have more status.
_____	9. I don't want to work full time.
_____	10. I want to improve my skills so I can get a better job.
_____	11. My parents gave me no other choice.
_____	12. I have a strong desire to achieve.
_____	13. I want to become more independent.
_____	14. I wanted to get away from home.
_____	15. I want to participate in campus social life.
_____	16. I have an athletic scholarship, veteran's benefits, etc.
_____	17. College graduates have better jobs.
_____	18. I couldn't go when I was younger.
_____	19. I can advance to a higher level position at work.
_____	20. To help ensure success in life.
_____	21. I want to please my family.
_____	22. I want to provide a good role model for my children.
_____	23. I am being retrained because I lost my job.

List 5 of your reasons in order of priority (1 = highest priority).

1. _____

2. _____

3. _____

4. _____

5. _____

▮ Exercise 2. Values

In the first column check 10 of the values that are most important to you. In the second column, rank from 1–10 the order of priority of these 10 values.

Value		
A world without prejudice	_____	_____
A satisfying and fulfilling marriage	_____	_____
Lifetime financial security	_____	_____
A really good love relationship	_____	_____
Unlimited travel opportunities	_____	_____
A complete library for your use	_____	_____
A lovely home in a beautiful setting	_____	_____
A happy family relationship	_____	_____
Good self-esteem	_____	_____
Freedom to do what you want	_____	_____
An understanding of the meaning of life	_____	_____
Success in your chosen profession	_____	_____
A peaceful world	_____	_____
Recognition as the most attractive person in the world	_____	_____
A satisfying religious faith	_____	_____
Freedom within your work setting	_____	_____
Tickets and travel to any cultural or athletic event as often as you wish	_____	_____
The love and admiration of friends	_____	_____
A chance to direct the destinies of a nation	_____	_____
International fame and popularity	_____	_____
The ability to eliminate sickness and poverty	_____	_____
A month's vacation with nothing to do but enjoy yourself	_____	_____

Write a brief paragraph describing what goals you are setting for yourself that reflects your top value choices.

_____

_____

_____

_____

_____

_____

_____

_____

Exercise 3. The Coat of Arms

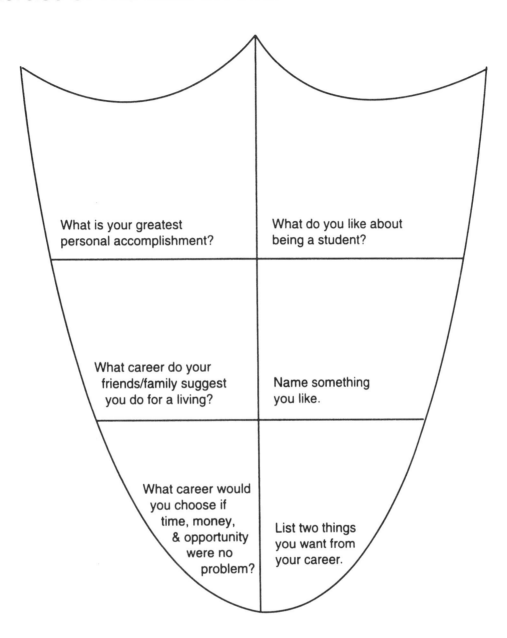

What is your greatest personal accomplishment?

What do you like about being a student?

What career do your friends/family suggest you do for a living?

Name something you like.

What career would you choose if time, money, & opportunity were no problem?

List two things you want from your career.

■ Exercise 4. Personal Goals

Your responses must meet the established criteria for goals!

Semester/quarter goals: _____

_____

_____

_____

Mid-term goals: _____

_____

_____

_____

One-year goals: _____

_____

_____

_____

Monthly goals: _____

_____

_____

_____

■ Exercise 5. External or Internal Motivation?

Considering your experience in classes that you have taken, what has motivated you to learn, to work, to achieve?

In the first column, put a check mark if the experience has been used to motivate you. In the second column, decide whether the motivation was *E* (external motivation) or *I* (internal motivation).

_____ _____ 1. Teacher paying attention to me

_____ _____ 2. Not wanting to disappoint the teacher

_____ _____ 3. Getting on the honor roll

_____ _____ 4. Getting a job in the future

_____ _____ 5. Wanting to learn and understand

_____ _____ 6. Parents caring about me

_____ _____ 7. Teacher caring about me

_____ _____ 8. My satisfaction from receiving a high grade on an exam

_____ _____ 9. Not wanting to disappoint parents

_____ _____ 10. Being praised by classmates

_____ _____ 11. Finally figuring out the correct answer

_____ _____ 12. Putting words together that became concepts that made sense

_____ _____ 13. Helping other students

_____ _____ 14. Pleasing my family

List below the latest internal motivator that you have experienced.

_____

List below the latest external motivator that you have experienced.

_____

Write a brief paragraph describing how you feel you became motivated. Do internal or external motivation factors seem to be the most important? Do you feel motivated at this time of your life? Why?

_____

_____

_____

_____

_____

_____

_____

_____

_____

CHAPTER 9 STRESS MANAGEMENT
Stressing the Point

Y ou are going to be faced with many academic and personal challenges during college. One key to meeting your challenges is to maintain a balanced life. A balance of academic, social, recreational, physical, and mental activities may be difficult to maintain, but it is necessary to your well-being. Your mind and body must be up to meeting the challenges that you will face as a student. Your academic success depends on your mental abilities, which are dependent on your physical well-being, which is dependent on your emotional health, which is dependent on your mental abilities, . . . and the cycle goes on. Your body, mind, and emotions are connected, and you must take care of each to take care of all of them.

From *Practical Approaches for Building Study Skills and Vocabulary*, Second Edition by Funk et al. © 1996 by Kendall/Hunt Publishing Company.

You must control the stress in your life in appropriate and positive ways if you are going to be a successful student. Handling stress in negative ways will make you an inefficient and ineffective student.

■ What Is Stress?

The word STRESS has a negative connotation to most of us, but that is probably incorrect when you look at the definition. Stress is the nonspecific result of any demand on the body. This definition was used by Dr. Hans Selye, M.D., who was a pioneer in the study of stress. Stress alone is not the problem, but how one copes with the stress can cause problems. Tension, worry, and anxiety may be ways to cope with stress, but those are the negative ways which result in negative effects on the body.

We are living in a time with more stress. Accepting that fact and learning coping strategies must be part of your education if you are going to be successful once you complete your education (and complete it as a successful student).

Stress is normal and useful because it can sharpen your awareness, give your energy a boost, and help you perform at your best. It's the way the body gets ready to adapt to change by releasing hormones to prepare us for adapting. Stress can be the result of pleasant as well as unpleasant circumstances. In fact, our bodies perceive excitement in almost the same manner as fear, with increased heart rate and flow of adrenaline and muscle contractions.

Stress may become a problem if it persists or becomes excessive. The best defense against stress is managing it in a positive way because no one can completely be free of stress. We all have situations and circumstances that cause us to feel stress. Learning how to cope with what happens and to control our reactions is essential to managing stress successfully.

If high levels of stress continue for long periods of time, negative effects will result. Tension, anxiety, and worry are the wrong responses to stress. They create the strain on your body and wear it out. Recent studies indicate that these reactions may depress your immune system and leave you vulnerable to viruses, as well as cause other physical ailments. Stress may interfere with your ability to mentally cope with problems and pressures. These negatives are what you need to learn to control. One of the first steps in learning to manage stress, tension, anxiety, and worry is to identify what causes you to have those feelings. Then, decide how to best manage them (or the stress associated with them).

■ Stressors

Stressors are (external and internal) events, conditions, situations, or people which make demands on you. They are what cause you to have stressful feelings. Stressors may be very different among individuals. Examples of stressors are examinations, instructors, assignments, commitments, money, family members, friends, and work. Your list may include others. A stressor may be a crisis, some positive change, or something minor, but it will require that you take some action or make some decision. Your management of stressors is important, and will be discussed throughout this chapter.

One stressor for many college students is procrastination. Procrastination is putting off doing a task to a later date or time. The common result is that the time left to do the task is not sufficient to do it well. This kind of tactic, on a regular basis will cause you to feel a lot of tension and worry. It may also cause your grade point average to be low.

The more tension and worry you feel, the less efficient and effective you become. This is a very difficult cycle to break. The best advice is to prevent the procrastination in the first place.

Certainly, negative events are thought of first as causing stress and tension, but positive things and changes can also cause stress. Things such as enrolling in college, moving, an outstanding personal achievement, vacation or holiday, marriage or becoming engaged, any changes in social activities or recreation, eating habits, or work hours or responsibilities can be stressors. Obviously, you would not want to avoid all changes and positive events in your life. However, if you are aware that you may experience stress because some of these have recently occurred in your life, you can be better prepared to cope with it. If you have experienced several negative and/or positive occurrences recently, you may be more susceptible to becoming ill or having an accident. Being aware of the times that you are more vulnerable to such things can help you take precautions.

Self-Esteem

Another area to be discussed along with stress and tension is low self-esteem. A healthy regard for yourself is necessary if you are going to do your best. This is another case where one thing influences many others. For example, if your academic performance suffers because of your low self-esteem (you are telling yourself that you can't perform well), then your self-esteem will suffer even more when you get the results of your poor academic performance (test or assignment grades). However, if you were telling yourself that you can do well (and putting in your best effort), you may see more positive academic results.

Low self-esteem is a major mental health problem in this country. Many psychologists and mental health professionals believe that it is at the core of many types of mental health problems: substance abuse, depression, eating disorders, etc.

Common Stressors of College Students

1. *Assignments and examinations*

2. *Time management (including procrastination and lack of time)*

3. *Academic failure (grades included)*

4. *Friends and relationships*

5. *Money*

6. *Family*

When college students were asked to list their most common stressors, they listed those above in rank order. Other areas listed less frequently were "bad habits" to change, lack of sleep, anxiety, future, and career goals. This is representative of what many students feel.

The amount of control you take over what happens in your life is generally influenced by self-esteem. The lower the self-esteem, the more likely you are to react negatively in situations or circumstances that should not cause you to feel tension. The higher the self-esteem, the more likely you are to do what is needed in the situation, and feel that you are in control.

Anxiety is an unpleasant apprehension directed at future events and self-doubt at the ability to cope with those events. Anxiety may be higher if your self-esteem is low. Anxiety, tension, and worry are the wrong responses to stress and will have negative effects on you and your performance. Low self-esteem is something to watch and keep in check, if you are going to learn to cope with stress in a positive way. After all, you have made it this far! Feel good about that, and focus on the things you do well. You will react to situations and events in a more positive way when your self-esteem is high. That will help you cope with stress in a more positive way, keeping the tension, worry, and anxiety to a minimum.

■ How Does Stress Affect You?

Stress affects both your mental and physical being. One aspect of the effects of stress is your academic performance. Since that may be uppermost on your list, we'll discuss it first. Keep in mind that you do need a little stress to adapt to changes and to perform at your best, but the stress effects presented here are caused by too much stress. We're actually talking about tension, worry, and anxiety (the inappropriate or negative ways of dealing with stress).

Most students want to be successful, and they want to learn. According to most, they want to finish their college educations by earning a degree. Being gainfully employed and possibly even doing something enjoyable would be the result of a college education. Many obstacles may come up along the way, and stress can be one that causes you to stumble and be less successful. Too much stress can affect your memory, concentration, and ability to perform academically.

When faced with a heavy academic load (as you will be as you try to learn everything you are expected to learn), you may feel stress caused by that academic load! When you are faced with an enormous amount of information to process and many facts to learn, you may feel tension if you have not been in the habit of learning and exercising your mind. Psychologists refer to this as cognitive stress. There is a change in the amount of learning you are expected to do, and this change triggers stress which may then result in feeling tension, worry, or anxiety. Your problem-solving ability may be negatively affected. This stress, on top of everything else, may hinder your academic performance.

Memory and Concentration

Obviously, your memory and concentration are important to your academic success. They may not work for you if you are experiencing too much stress. The negative effects on your memory are twofold: First, you may not be able to receive information best if your mind is cluttered with tension and worry. A relaxed mind seems to accept new information better, and the information has a better chance of staying in your memory. Second, you can't retrieve information from a tense mind as well as one that is relaxed. This causes problems at study time and at test time!

EXAMPLE: Have you ever been asked for the title of a song, or book, or someone's name, and you can't think of it? Most of us try harder to remember and cause ourselves to get tense, but information doesn't come. Then, after you have relaxed and put the whole thing out of your mind, the information comes to you! It comes to you when you have a relaxed mind—when you have gotten rid of the tension.

The example demonstrates the retrieving problem with memory. The receiving problem can best be illustrated by the following example: You are late going somewhere important, and you don't know how to get to the appointment. You are tense about being late, and because you don't know where you are. When you stop and ask directions, you think you understand and remember them, but you forget the name of the street, which way to turn on it, or how many blocks. The information didn't "catch" in your memory because you were tense, and your mind was cluttered with negative thoughts.

This illustration also shows the problems tension can cause with concentration. It's difficult to concentrate when you are tense or worried. Concentration is essential when you read a textbook and listen to a lecture. If you can't concentrate, you can't get the information you need—from reading or listening.

> **Critical Thinking**
>
> *Think for a moment about some of the problems that invade your mind when you're trying to concentrate on reading a textbook or listening to a lecture. Perhaps you can come up with a signal or word to yourself that will get you back on track immediately. Give yourself time later to think about the problem.*

Test Stress

If you can't remember or concentrate, you are probably going to have trouble at test time. Test anxiety is a specific kind of stress, and can cause major problems for you if you don't learn to cope with it. Most of your academic performance is determined by your test scores, so you have to learn to control test anxiety and do well on tests.

Stress may cause you to have problems studying to learn new information or you may have difficulty retrieving it at test time. Either problem is one you must control to be a successful student.

Personal Life

Stress also affects your personal life, your emotions, your relationships, and your health. Those, in turn, affect your ability to be an effective and efficient student. The personal aspects of stress will be discussed later in this chapter, along with the impact of not coping with stress in appropriate ways. Stress can cause psychological problems for you, and psychological problems can cause more stress.

Academic achievement and success in your personal life are closely tied together. Experience problems in one area and you probably have problems in the other area. Stress, tension, worry, and anxiety can be caused by either academic problems or personal problems; they can also make problems worse. You may cease to deal with problems in a sensible way when you become overwhelmed. Problem-solving, decision-making, and the ability to organize are only a few areas where you may find yourself being less effective.

How Do You Know If You Are Experiencing Too Much Stress?

Most of us have our own "gauges" that tell us when we're not coping well. (Your results to the "Stress Index" would be useful here.) Take a minute to look at the following list of symptoms that may indicate that your stress level is too high.

The "Mental" Signs

Irritability
Depression
Low productivity
Strained relationships (with family, friends, co-workers)
Feeling burned-out (with school, work, other activities)
Feeling tense or anxious
Nervousness for no apparent reason
Forgetfulness
Concentration problems
Patterns of avoiding tasks

The "Physical" Signs

Upset stomach
Frequent colds
Low energy
Change in sleep pattern
Fatigue
Change in eating habits (significant weight loss or gain)
Tense muscles (especially in the neck, back, shoulders)
Muscle aches
Change in smoking or alcohol intake

There may be many reasons for those symptoms including actual physical ailments needing medical attention. If the physical reasons are ruled out, and if you have experienced several of the symptoms recently, unmanaged stress may be the underlying reason.

If these symptoms are left unchecked, you may find yourself with more serious psychological or physical problems. Psychologically, you may experience emotional instability, mood swings, apathy, deep depression, or mental and physical fatigue that leave you unable to cope. You may feel out of control and your self-worth may suffer.

Physically, you may experience a more serious version of the physical problems mentioned, or you may suffer from high blood pressure, cardiovascular problems, skin problems, digestive disorders (ulcers), or severe headaches (migraines), to mention only a few. These health problems and others associated with stress are real and can have very serious long-term effects.

Be aware of your own physical and mental "gauges" of too much stress. When you see a problem, ask yourself the following questions to determine whether it is stress induced:

1. Are the symptoms not responding well to regular treatment?

2. Did the problem begin right after or during a major life change?

3. Are you having a combination of mental and physical problems?

4. Do you have difficulty getting up in the morning?

5. Are you feeling out-of-control?

Unacceptable Behavior

People may begin to act in socially unacceptable ways or exhibit maladaptive behaviors as coping mechanisms. Often, there are serious consequences resulting from bad decisions made under stress. Good decision-making requires that you be able to look at the options you have and choose the one that appears to be the best. People under a lot of stress may not be able to look at all of the options or see the options objectively. They may avoid making decisions or make them without considering the consequences carefully.

Unfortunately, suicide may be one of the bad decisions a person makes because they can't cope with what's going on in their lives. Suicide numbers have been rising over the last several years. The number of young people attempting and committing suicide has risen sharply. Someone has said that if people were dying from a disease at the same rate as the young are committing suicide, it would be considered an epidemic.

Most people who commit suicide are not mentally ill, they are just extremely unhappy. Depression and feelings of worthlessness are factors which influence a person to attempt suicide. Substance abuse may be a contributing factor. These people are crying out for attention and may see suicide as the ultimate revenge or a way of taking control of a situation that seems uncontrollable. Most have given warnings or talked about committing suicide before attempting it. Following is a list of signs that may indicate a person is considering suicide:

1. School performance falling drastically

2. Withdrawn, uncommunicative attitude

3. Disruptive or unruly behavior

4. Giving away personal articles

5. Talking about suicide

6. Shifts in eating, sleeping, or drinking patterns

Early detection of those who may be considering suicide is the main prevention. With the proper treatment, the person can be helped to overcome the helpless feelings. Family, friends, and counselors can guide the person to a positive way to deal with problems.

As you have seen from the information presented, there is a definite relationship between your mind and body.

■ What Is the Relationship between Mind and Body?

Your physical self, emotional/mental self, and social self will be discussed in this section. You cannot separate the parts from the person—you cannot take one part away and continue to function. The parts must be seen as being interdependent on each other, not independent. There must be a balance of the parts for the whole thing (you) to function properly. Abusing or neglecting any area will likely cause you to have problems, not only in that area, but others as well.

When referring to the physical self, the following factors are important: nutrition, fitness, stress management, avoidance of harmful substances, safe sex, and illness. When referring to the emotional/mental self, the following are included: feelings, life's purpose, adapting to change, thoughts, worries, and personality tendencies. When referring to the social self, the following will be discussed: relationships and the way you relate to others.

The idea of taking care of yourself with regard to each area may be a problem at times. The following suggestions and information will help you make decisions based on keeping the balance in your life. Think of this as a holistic approach to academics. You will find it very difficult to be academically successful and have problems in the areas mentioned above.

■ Physical Self

Your body is where the rest of the parts are housed. You can think of it as a machine, and if it isn't running properly, the other parts may not work properly. Your body needs nutrition, exercise, and rest. It sounds simple, yet many times we neglect even those areas. To a large extent you can choose your level of health by the choices you make about nutrition, exercise, and rest. Of course, we all have to live with what we have—which is less than perfect for most of us, but the "machine" we have cannot be replaced. It stands to reason that you should take care of this one.

Exercise and Activity

One of the essential ingredients to having the machine working at its best is exercise. Physical activity is needed to relieve stress and tension and keep your muscles in shape. Exercise releases chemicals in your brain (endorphins) which actually make you feel better!

Critical Thinking

AEROBIC WORKOUT: Three 20–30 minute sessions per week of aerobic activity are recommended for best results. To be considered aerobic, the activity must elevate your heart rate and maintain it. There must be continuous muscular activity for the entire 20 or 30 minutes. Check with a doctor or someone who knows about physical workouts for the heart rate you should maintain for the best results. You should always check with a physician before beginning any exercise program.

The only way to have lean muscles (and therefore a lean body) is to exercise. Your mind will also function better when your body is in shape and functioning well. Activity can be an appropriate way to work off tension; channeling energy into a physical activity will often relieve some of the stress your mind and body are experiencing. It may even increase your life expectancy.

There are any number of opportunities and places for exercise and activity. You probably have the option of different sports at the intramural level, sports clubs and activities, courses, and facilities for swimming, running, and weight training. There are probably others, and you need to decide what suits you best. You may prefer individual activities like bicycling, jogging, or swimming. Walking is an excellent form of exercise that can be done in most places with little special equipment (walking shoes).

Nutrition

Nutrition is an area often neglected by college students, but like exercise, it's important if you want to function at your best mentally and physically. Nutrition habits that you develop now can be important to your future health. Good nutrition habits include eating the right foods and eating the right amount of food. There are four general guidelines to follow to ensure that you eat the "right" things:

1. Eat a variety of foods each day (fruits, vegetables, whole grains, dairy products)

2. Increase starch and fiber consumption

3. Decrease fat and cholesterol consumption

4. Decrease salt and sugar consumption

If you follow these guidelines, you should be close to eating the proper foods. Obviously, nutrition is more complicated, but remember the balance idea discussed previously—it applies here also.

By the way, your mom isn't here to make you get up in time to eat breakfast, but you should. A balanced breakfast is necessary to get you started in the morning. Sugar, fat, cholesterol, and caffeine are not the four food groups to be included in a healthy breakfast!

The other nutrition consideration is eating the proper amount of food. Two eating disorders, anorexia nervosa and bulimia are tied to the amount of food eaten. Anorexia is characterized by extended fasting or eating very little. Bulimia, on the other hand, is characterized by eating huge amounts of food (binging) and getting rid of the food (purging) by vomiting, using laxatives, enemas, or diuretics. Both are a very serious problem and can cause long-term damage to the body.

Many people have a tendency to eat too much on occasion, but when it becomes a lifestyle, weight gain will be the result. Gaining weight occurs when you take in more calories than you use. Your body stores the unused calories as fat. College life may mean sitting in the classroom, sitting in the library, and sitting in your room. In other words, your activity may be less than before, and you may see yourself gaining weight. The answer may be as simple as increasing your activity and decreasing the amount of food you eat (or changing high fat foods for those with less fat).

Rest

Nutrition and activity are essential to keep your machine running, but so is rest. More sleep is often something college students wish they could get. Sleep is one thing that we think we can neglect or put off until later and get by. That isn't true. The drastic and extreme deprivation of sleep can literally drive you crazy, and perhaps cause death. You probably aren't doing that to yourself, but lack of restful sleep can prevent you from putting in your best performance.

How much sleep should you have? Your body will probably let you know how much you need. Different people may have different needs. There's some controversy about the number of hours of sleep needed on a regular basis. Most of us need at least 6 hours and many people need up to 12 hours to feel their best. You probably have some idea of the amount you require. If not, try differing amounts of sleep over a long period of time to see when you feel best. Many people also find that they function better when getting up at approximately the same time each day. Be aware of your sleep needs and patterns.

One word of caution regarding sleep; although the more common problem is not getting enough, you may find that you are sleeping too much. Sleep can be a way to avoid problems or tasks that need attention. Restful sleep is essential if you are going to wake up feeling refreshed and rested. Managing stress, and keeping your life balanced will help you get the restful sleep necessary.

Signs of Not Getting the Proper Amount of Restful Sleep

1. Depression

2. Irritability

3. Constant fatigue

4. Emotional problems

5. Mood swings

6. Falling asleep in class

■ Harmful Substances

The focus has been on what you can do to ensure that you are treating the physical part of you well. Now, the focus shifts to the effects of substances which can be very harmful to you (physically and mentally). The ingestion of substances (alcohol and other drugs) as a way of coping with stress is uniquely human. It's also temporary because the illusion created by the substance fades as the substance wears off.

The terms "substance" and "drug" will be used interchangeably here. The definition to be used for either term will be broad and will include alcohol, nicotine (tobacco), illicit substances, prescription medicines, and caffeine. Any misuse or abuse of these chemicals can cause serious problems.

Whether to use any substance is a complicated issue. It's complicated even more by the fact that some of the drugs are legal and some are illegal. Another complication is the difference between use and abuse, and the risk of using any substance is that you will become addicted to the substance (addiction can be physical or psychological). You must decide for yourself whether the pay-off is worth the risk. The pay-off generally is that "getting high" feels good—it's fun or people wouldn't do it!

The underlying reasons for people using drugs may include the need to be accepted, lack of confidence, low self-esteem, the desire to rebel, and relaxation. The financial cost of using drugs may be the most obvious problem; along with the legal problems associated with using an illegal substance. Being arrested for driving while under the influence of alcohol or another drug is a serious crime. The less obvious problems such as the harm done to your body and the problems associated with abuse and addiction may not be so apparent to you as you make decisions about whether to use drugs.

On college campuses, illicit drug use has apparently declined since the late 1970s. The "drug of choice" on most campuses is alcohol, with cigarettes being the second choice, and marijuana the third. You probably will come in contact with people who are using drugs, and you will have to make decisions regarding your use. One of the important things to consider is that you run the risk of becoming physically or mentally addicted, and it is very difficult to change addictions. There is convincing evidence that addiction to alcohol and tobacco is no different than an addiction to any other drug—those two just happen to be legal.

Alcohol

Research indicates that many people make decisions about drinking while in high school. In college the amount of alcohol may increase, but more likely the frequency will increase. This is especially true for the person who is a "binge" drinker. (Binge drinking is drinking 5 or more drinks in a row). The lack of supervision, more time available, more independence, and the inability to make responsible decisions about alcohol contribute to the increased frequency of drinking.

Drinking on weekends and with friends is the most reported way that college students drink. Drinking is considered a "social" activity, but peer pressure to participate is not necessarily the main reason for drinking. Those who drink are usually aware of the consequences and have had problems as a result of their drinking—both personal and legal problems. Consider all sides of the issue when making your decision about drinking. It is more complicated than "just saying no" for most.

Tobacco, Caffeine, and Marijuana

Tobacco and caffeine are legal drugs, but you should think seriously about your use of them (see the chart below). Being addicted to nicotine is a very difficult addiction to stop, and the health risks to yourself and those around you are monumental. In fact, if college (or anything else) was considered as dangerous as smoking, the colleges would be empty!

Cigarette and Tobacco Information

- *A smoker is 25 times more likely to be involved in an accident.*

- *Smokers have 50 percent more accidents and 46 percent more traffic violations.*

- *Smoking is the #1 cause of preventable death.*

- *1 out of 7 deaths in the U.S. is caused by smoking.*

- *Smoking kills more than AIDS, heroin, crack, cocaine, alcohol, car accidents, fire, and murder combined.*

- *The tobacco industry needs at least 1,000 new smokers per day to replace those who die from smoking.*

- *Since 1980, cigarette smoking has been higher in females than males in college.*

- *Crib death occurs 2½ more times among babies of smoking mothers.*

- *If you live with a smoker, you have a 20% greater risk of cancer.*

- *1 hour in a smoke-filled room is equivalent to smoking 1 cigarette.*

- *Passive (second-hand) smoke is the third leading cause of preventable death.*

- *Thousands of non-smokers die each year from second-hand smoke.*

- *The relapse rate after quitting cigarettes is the same as for heroin and cocaine addicts (3 out of 4 relapse by one year).*

- *Most smokers have to quit an average of 5 times before they are successful.*

Caffeine in coffee, tea, chocolate, colas, and some over-the-counter medicines is not the major health issue as some of the previously discussed substances, but it should be viewed as a drug. Using caffeine to stay awake is no substitute for getting enough restful sleep. The health risks associated with caffeine are still being discussed by the experts.

Marijuana is one of the more prevalent illegal drugs used by college students. Aside from the legal concerns, there are other problems associated with continued use. Those of major concern to students are the negative effects on memory and learning.

The image of college life which includes spending all of the time drinking and partying is probably about as far from the truth as the image of spending all of the time in class and studying. For most students, it takes awhile to feel comfortable in the new surroundings with new freedom to choose how their time will be spent. Your choices are important and should be made with the thought that they will affect your future. Ask yourself whether the risks are worth the pay-offs.

You cannot separate your mental and physical selves. What you put into the physical self (food, harmful substances) will effect your mental self. The next section will focus on two more examples of the interrelationships of the mental and physical by looking at relationships (including sex) and your personality tendencies.

■ Relationships

Relationships can cause you stress if they aren't going well, but they can also help you deal with your stress. If you recall, relationships and friends were listed as a stressor by college students. One of the first things that you may want to do if you are having trouble with relationships is to examine yourself. Are you the kind of person someone would want to have any sort of relationship with? If you consistently have trouble, YOU may be the problem. Your general attitudes and feelings, along with changing some of your thinking, may help.

Your well-being depends somewhat on the meaningful relationships that you are able to establish and maintain. One old cliche that holds a lot of truth is the one about not being able to love someone else until you love yourself. You must also take responsibility for your feelings, thoughts, and actions.

There will be many events and circumstances over which you have little or no control. You CAN control the way you react. If you cannot change a person or situation, the only alternative is to change the way you feel about it, or at least the way you outwardly react. This is often a necessary way to deal with people and the problems involved in getting along. Taking control of your emotions can begin by understanding what causes you to feel a certain way. The next step would be to take responsibility for those feelings instead of "giving" it to someone else. Look at the following sets of statements. Those on the left are examples of giving someone else responsibility, and those on the right are examples of your taking responsibility for the way you feel.

You make me angry when you . . .	I feel angry when you . . .
He makes me happy . . .	I feel happy because he . . .
She disappointed me . . .	I feel disappointed when . . .
They frustrate me . . .	I am frustrated when . . .

Making the statements on the left is common to most of us, but the ones on the right are what you should strive for because, in these, you are "owning" the feeling and taking responsibility for it. This is a better way to communicate with someone about your feelings. It shows that you are responsible for your feelings, and you aren't giving someone else that responsibility.

When considering past or present problems you may be having with relationships, one of the things that may come to mind is a problem with communication. It seems to be common. Consider the following ideas when you want to communicate: LISTEN AND BE SUPPORTIVE. Listening is an active process, and when you are communicating with someone, you should be listening part of the time and talking part of the time (not delivering a monologue)! Being supportive means joining in with the other person's triumphs and troubles, and communicating that support. You cannot assume that the other person knows about your support.

As you come in contact with new people, you may find the following suggestions helpful: keep your expectations realistic, make yourself available to listen and participate in activities, give in occasionally on unimportant issues, and give the other person a break. Viewing life as a competition is going to cause you problems, because cooperation is the key to getting along. Both competition and cooperation are contagious, so consider which atmosphere you would prefer. Being uncomfortable with so many new people is not unusual. Understanding that others have insecurities can help you overcome yours.

Are you someone others want to be around? If so, great! If not, maybe you should consider some changes in your problem areas. Accepting the fact that change is needed is a step in the right direction.

■ Safe Sex

Many students come to college with unrealistic expectations regarding relationships. The expectations may be in the form of assuming that friends will be made immediately with little or no effort, or that this is the place and time when a life partner will be found, or that there will be a constant stream of dates. While some of those expectations may become reality, for most they don't, and they certainly don't on the first day!

Another expectation concerns sex. Some feel that being in college ensures that there will be lots of sexual activity. Unrealistic expectations about sex can mean problems. Consider the following information when making your choices about sex. The possible problems are unwanted pregnancies, sexually transmitted diseases (STDs), and emotional issues.

Being aware of the problems can help you make good choices. If you choose to have sex, protecting yourself against those problems is necessary. Whether or not to have sex is your choice. It is never O.K. to force someone to have sex, and you always have the right to refuse to have sex. Rape is a serious crime, whether the rapist is known by you or unknown.

■ "Personality Types"

Since the mid 1970s a particular "personality type" has been associated closely with coronary problems. Drs. Meyer Friedman and Ray Rosenman described this behavior pattern and called it Type A. The contrasting behavior pattern is called Type B.

Type A Characteristics	*Type B Characteristics*
Aggressiveness	Relaxed attitude
Competitiveness	Easily satisfied
Impatience	Unhurried
Chronically trying to do more in less time	Not constantly trying to do more
Easily aroused to anger	Rarely being angry
Doing more than one thing at a time	Less concerned with achievement
Being tense	

Which person would you rather work with? Live with? Although the tendencies to react a certain way may be deeply ingrained in each of us, we can change. Some may wonder which set of behaviors one would want to change. If you're wondering that, you may have just answered the question of which behavior pattern you have—A! About 50 percent of the U.S. population is Type A; about 40 percent Type B; and the remaining 10 percent show characteristics of both.

Type A behavior patterns are problems because they will increase your risk of stress related illnesses such as heart disease and high blood pressure. Relaxing is difficult for the Type A and their bodies tend to wear out a little quicker (sometimes a lot quicker).

You can still be a person who wants to achieve and be successful. The problem is with the anger, hostility, and tension the Type A person keeps as a constant companion.

Type B behavior patterns may appear to be at odds with success and achievement, but that's not true. This person just has a different attitude about it. That attitude allows for relaxing and working at a task without being competitive. The goal is not to make everyone a Type B, but for the Type A to learn to control the excessive behavior, learn to relax and slow down some.

■ How Can You Appropriately Handle Stress?

The consequences of not coping with stress are detrimental to your mental and physical health, and will cause problems with your academic success. Realizing that you need to find appropriate ways to deal with stress is the first step in finding those strategies which will help you.

Several ways to cope with stress will be presented. The mental and physical relationship is essential in coping with stress, so both mental and physical strategies will be offered. Strategies for eliminating stress and for controlling or coping with stress are presented, in the hope that you can find several strategies which will work for you. Be aware that there are times when it is appropriate and necessary to get help from someone.

Reducing Stress

Two of the essential attitudes in reducing the amount of stress you have are to feel 1) that you are in control of your life—that you have a self-directed lifestyle and 2) that you can cope with any problems that you encounter. This means taking responsibility for your actions, decisions, feelings, reactions, and thoughts. It's very important to your mental and physical health to come to these realizations. No doubt, there will be situations and circumstances which you cannot control, but remember that you CAN control your reactions, feelings, and decisions regarding those situations or circumstances. You can make good decisions and choices.

Believing that you have control over your life requires that you also believe that you can cope with problems that you encounter. You have probably faced and solved many problems up to this point. Just getting this far (to college) has produced problems that you have satisfactorily solved. Worrying about problems is often the cause for added tension and stress. Eliminate the worry and you lessen the stress. Believing in yourself and your ability to handle your problems is a major step in the right direction, but remember to get help if you need it.

Avoiding Stressors

Avoiding stressors is sometimes an appropriate way to lessen your stress level. You can't avoid examinations and assignments, or some people, but you can possibly improve your attitude about what you can't avoid entirely. You can avoid stressors such as lack of preparation for examinations and assignments. In fact, if you really want to lessen your stress on academic tasks, be overprepared. Test anxiety will be less severe if you have prepared well for the test questions. An assignment can cause stress, but probably a greater producer of stress for college students is procrastination. As discussed earlier, take care of this problem, and you will lower your stress level.

Decision Making

Effective Decision Making

1. *Looking at alternatives*

2. *Looking at objectives to be met by decision*

3. *Looking at and weighing the consequences of a decision*

4. *Searching out alternatives*

5. *Considering new alternatives and possible effects on the decision*

6. *Making plans to carry out the decision and a contingency plan if the decision does not work*

Negative Effects of Stress on Decision Making

1. *Choosing to make no decision*

2. *Making changes with no contingency plans*

3. *Making decisions without considering enough options*

4. *Continuing to search for alternatives, but not making a decision*

5. *Choosing an alternative that is not the best one*

You have many demands placed on you as a college student, and you must be realistic regarding what you can and can't do. Striving for perfection is a sure way to set yourself up for disappointment. The superhuman image is unhealthy and unrealistic. Realistically look at what you have to do and set priorities based on what's most important to you and your future. Give yourself permission to make mistakes. Mistakes become large problems when you continue to make them again and again, or you choose to dwell on them. Be reasonable with yourself—most of us won't do everything well, and we certainly won't do things right the first time! Striving for excellence, not perfection, is much more realistic. It's also easier for most of us to achieve! Your energy can best be used changing what you can, and accepting what you can't change! When you make a less than desirable choice or don't live up to what you thought you should have done, remember it's only one event—you're still O.K. Failure is an event, not a person. You should evaluate what you did and didn't do correctly and leave it behind you.

Tension Relievers

Even if you are doing your best to lower the inappropriate stress in your life, you will have times that you need strategies to release or relieve stress. There are numerous suggestions for relieving stress and many are very good, some are not. This list is a compilation from several sources, but it is not a complete list of good ideas. You may have discovered some very good ones on your own. As long as the method is not harmful to you or others and is (somewhat) socially acceptable, continue to use it. Here are suggestions that you may want to try.

1. Be aware of the times that you are under stress and what causes you to feel tension.

2. Talk about your problems with someone. Talking to someone often helps you get a different perspective on your problem and helps you find a solution or plan. Even if no solution comes from the discussion, you are likely to feel better just verbalizing the problem (also remember to be a good listener when someone else needs to talk).

3. Have realistic goals for yourself. Setting your goals too high or too low can cause disappointment and frustration.

Action Plan to Eliminate Stress

1. *Identify the cause of stress.*

2. *Determine if this is* really *the source of stress (you must find the real source of stress).*

3. *Can you avoid the stressor? If not, think of ways you can control your reaction to it, and practice the strategies.*

4. *When you feel stressful (tension, anxiety, worry), try some of the suggestions given in this chapter for relieving stress.*

4. Learn to accept what you cannot change. If you can't change it, change your thinking about it.

5. Deal with your anger. Chronic, pent-up anger is unhealthy. Working it off or channeling it into some acceptable physical activity is a good solution. When you must deal with a situation while you are angry, try to appear calm on the outside, and you will find yourself calming on the inside.

6. Take time for relaxation and recreation. Learn how to relax. You need to schedule or plan time for the things that you enjoy doing. Recreation is not a waste of time. Hobbies and activities allow us time to put aside our worries, tension, and anxieties, and come back ready to meet the challenges.

7. Plan tasks so you can handle them. Make lists of what should be done and prioritize them. Take them one at a time, or you will be overwhelmed. Check off what you accomplish. Learn to refuse obligations and requests if necessary. You have time to do what's important to you!

8. Get away for awhile—either physically or mentally. If you can't actually physically leave, take a "mental" trip by imagining yourself in another place, doing something else.

9. Do something for someone else. This will take your mind off your problems, and you will be rewarded with a good feeling because you did something for someone. Your attitude will probably improve if you look around at others' problems.

10. Avoid self-medication. Don't fall into the trap of using alcohol or drugs to relieve your stress.

11. Look after your body. Get the required sleep, exercise, and nutritious food. Your body will not accept abuse without consequences.

Relaxation exercises and techniques have proven helpful in relieving and releasing tension. Most require a combination of relaxing your body by using your mind. Therefore, both become relaxed and have a respite from tension. There are many books and audio and video tapes with more detailed programs which you may want to investigate. Here are a few simple ones to try.

Following are two breathing exercises which you may find useful when you are in a situation that is causing you a lot of anxiety or tension (such as examinations or presentations).

1. Breathe in until you cannot hold any more air. Then, take a quick gasp of air through your mouth.

2. Breathe out very slowly.

Repeat as often as you need until you feel more relaxed.

1. Inhale slowly through your nose while silently counting to 4.

2. Hold your breath for a count of 4.

3. Exhale slowly through your nose to a count of 4.

4. With your breath out, count to 4.

5. Repeat the exercise as often as needed until you are relaxed. Count slowly through each step. Once you have the rhythm down, you don't have to continue counting.

The following are relaxation exercises to use when you need to feel more relaxed. You can use these instead of taking a nap.

1. Drop your head down close to your chest.

2. Very slowly rotate your neck all the way around.

3. Think only of your rotating neck. Concentrate on any tight or sore places. Try to relax these tight places.

4. Repeat several times until you feel your neck and head relax.

1. Lie down on the floor on your back.

2. Close your eyes and get comfortable—cross your ankles, fold your hands across your chest or behind your head, or get a pillow—whatever is more comfortable for you.

3. Lie completely still with eyes closed.

4. Focus *only* on your body.

5. Locate any tight muscles or sore spots. Concentrate on those spots, one at a time. Think of the uncomfortable area getting heavy. Move on to the next area of your body that feels tight or uncomfortable and repeat this step.

6. When all areas are comfortable and relaxed, begin to concentrate only on your feet. Let them begin to feel heavy.

7. Move up your body in slow stages, letting each area feel heavy: ankles, calf muscles, knees, thighs, hips, hands, lower arms, upper arms, shoulders, neck, and finally facial muscles.

8. Now, just relax. Your whole body should feel heavy and relaxed.

To get the full benefit from any of these exercises, concentrate on relaxing and tensing muscles, or breathing, or counting. Both your mind and body will feel refreshed after trying some of these exercises.

Throughout this section, suggestions have been given for managing stress. The first step in handling stress is to recognize when you are experiencing an inappropriate level of stress, and then to make changes in your lifestyle to accommodate the problem.

You may normally do a very good job of handling stress, but there are times when it is appropriate to seek help. Any number of places may offer you help for a particular problem. The following list is simply a beginning point.

Campus Counseling Center
Health Services
Campus Organizations

Residence Hall Assistants
Instructors
Friends
Community Agencies
Community Clinics
Books, Audio and Video Tapes
Yellow pages for listings of groups and other sources of help

Your overall stress management plan should include eliminating or reducing the stress you have and ways to cope with stress you will encounter. When you believe that you are in control of your life, and that you can solve your problems, you will be preventing some stress. Telling yourself these things is important to do because you will begin to believe them (if you don't already). Visualizing yourself being successful may increase the probability of positive results. Helping yourself with the mental and physical effects of stress is essential.

■ Summary

Stress is the body's way of getting ready for adapting to changes. It isn't always a negative influence, and can even be caused by positive events. The problems develop when a high level of stress is felt at inappropriate times, or the feeling is sustained for long periods of time. Stress affects the ability to remember and concentrate, which are important to academic success. It also affects mental and physical health. The body and mind are interdependent, and it is likely that problems in one area will cause problems in another area. Both mind and body must be taken care of, and attention given to any problem areas. Taking care of each (mind and body) will ensure that you are taking care of both.

The elimination of stress is probably not possible, but there are ways to reduce stress. Preventing stress is the key to managing it, and finding appropriate ways to release tension are necessary. Coping with stress is important to your academic success, physical health, and emotional well-being. Many of the lifestyle choices made now will remain with you, so good decisions about the way you will live your life are essential to continued success.

Name: _____ Date: _____

■ Stressor Worksheet

1. List the situations, people, circumstances, etc., which cause *you* stress.

_____

_____

_____

_____

_____

2. Now, go back and look at your list. You may want to do any or all of the following with the items listed.

   a. Number the stressors in order of the level of stress caused.

   b. Check off the items over which you have little or no control. These are the ones which may require that you learn to deal with them by controlling your reactions.

   c. Mark the ones which you *can* control (by changing something you are doing/not doing, by avoiding, or any other appropriate action). How can you make changes to lessen the stress you feel?

3. Choose one or two of these stressors, and come up with a workable plan to decrease the amount of stress caused by the item(s).

_____

_____

_____

_____

_____

_____

_____

■ What Is Your Stress Index?

Do You Frequently: **Yes**   **No**

1. Neglect your diet?   _____   _____

2. Try to do everything yourself?   _____   _____

3. Blow up easily?   _____   _____

4. Seek unrealistic goals?   _____   _____

5. Fail to see the humor in situations others find funny?   _____   _____

6. Act rude?   _____   _____

7. Make a "big deal" of everything?   _____   _____

8. Look to other people to make things happen?   _____   _____

9. Have difficulty making decisions?   _____   _____

10. Complain you are disorganized?   _____   _____

11. Avoid people whose ideas are different from your own?   _____   _____

12. Keep everything inside?   _____   _____

13. Neglect exercise?   _____   _____

14. Have only a few supportive relationships?   _____   _____

15. Use psychoactive drugs, such as sleeping pills and   _____   _____
    tranquilizers, without physician approval?

16. Get too little rest?   _____   _____

17. Get angry when you are kept waiting?   _____   _____

18. Ignore stress symptoms?   _____   _____

19. Procrastinate?   _____   _____

20. Think there is only one right way to do something?   _____   _____

21. Fail to build in relaxation time?   _____   _____

22. Gossip?   _____   _____

23. Race through the day?   _____   _____

24. Spend a lot of time lamenting the past?   _____   _____

25. Fail to get a break from noise and crowds?   _____   _____

■ What Your Score Means

Score 1 for each "yes" answer, 0 for each "no." Total your score.

1–6 There are few hassles in your life. Make sure, though, that you aren't trying so hard to avoid problems that you shy away from challenges.

7–13 You've got your life in pretty good control. Work on the choices and habits that could still be causing some unnecessary stress in your life.

14–20 You're approaching the danger zone. You may well be suffering stress-related symptoms and your relationships could be strained. Think carefully about choices you've made and take relaxation breaks every day.

Above 20 Emergency! You must stop now, rethink how you are living, change your attitudes, and pay scrupulous attention to your diet, exercise, and relation programs.

Worry Worksheet

List the upcoming events, assignments, situations, problems, etc., about which you are worried.

Worries

_____

_____

_____

_____

_____

_____

_____

_____

Go back and look at your list, and rank the items, giving the one that is *your* biggest worry a #1, the second a #2, on down your list.

Suggestions for dealing with the worries listed:

1. Choose a specific day and time that you will do nothing but worry about the items on your list. That is the *only* time that you can worry about them.

2. Choose one and write down a specific plan to do something about it. Include deadlines for yourself.

3. Imagine the worst thing that could happen if each of your listed items happens. Then give a percent to the probability of that "worst case scenario" happening.

Worry Information

Leo Buscaglia says that 90 percent of what you worry about never happens.

It's such a waste to spend $10 worth of energy on a 10 cent problem.

Only 8–10 percent of what we worry about turns out to be a legitimate problem.

CHAPTER 10 CASE STUDIES
Designated Driver
Case Study

Designated Driver

This case depicts the plight of a young freshman in the first week at college when he sees the designated driver for his group of friends drinking beer at the party they were attending. When the party is over and everyone is piling into the jeep for the ride back to campus, he wonders if the driver is really OK to drive and whether it is safe for him to climb in for the ride.

■ Designated Driver

Scott Duncan had just left the fraternity party and stood by the jeep as his friends climbed in. He was sure that none of them were sober enough to drive, but they piled in, laughing and shouting for him to hurry up. He had come with them and now, in a moment's hesitation, he wondered to himself, "Are these guys too drunk?"

First Week as a Freshman

The first week of college at Southern Tech was filled with social opportunities for Scott, a new freshman. He looked like many of his classmates: blonde hair, medium build, average dresser; but was shorter than most at only 5'4". Scott felt like he was entering college with a more mature attitude toward his new independence, compared to the way he saw many of his new friends act. He had made friends with most of the guys on his hall, and they had spent almost every night going out together to parties and clubs. This was a new experience for Scott, and he knew that once classes began, this type of socializing would have to cease. He came to Tech on almost a full scholarship, so he told himself that he would give himself this first week to get all of the partying out of his system so he could focus on his studies for the remainder of the semester.

The party scene was also pretty unfamiliar to Scott. He was not a big drinker in high school. In fact, he was a member of Teen Institute, a teen drug and alcohol prevention program. He had found himself in social drinking situations before, but had usually ended up having to "baby-sit" his friends. He did not consider himself a big party person in high school, and remembered getting drunk only twice; one time, ironically, at a medical leadership conference. Scott did not drink much, but he definitely considered himself a social person and someone who liked to have a good time.

The Fraternity Party

That first weekend, Scott's hallmate, Mike Spenser, invited him and several other guys on his hall to attend an Eta Rho Lambda fraternity party. Some of his hallmates were thinking about rushing this fraternity, so this party gave them the opportunity to meet some of the members and make connections. Scott had not really thought about rushing a fraternity, but this seemed like another good social opportunity before classes began. Scott was very conscious about drunk driving, so he made sure that one of the guys going with them promised to stay sober. Mike volunteered to be the designated driver for the evening. So, Scott and six other guys headed over to the Lambda party, which was being held at the fraternity's off-campus party house. It was about a two-mile drive which took them seven minutes to arrive.

They hopped out of the jeep and headed up the walk to the two-story house. The party was an open house; a chance for everyone to meet each other. Scott was in awe at the amount of beer being served—there must have been 12 kegs lined up against the wall. He felt a little out of place, not really knowing what to do at a fraternity open house. He was underage, but they assured him that he would not be carded to get a beer. He would just have to give a brother his cup and they would fill it up—it was just that simple.

The Designated Driver

Before they left for the party, Scott asked Mike three times if he was sure he wanted to stay sober. Mike assured him that he did. Now, after Scott got his first beer, he noticed that Mike had a cup in his hand. He approached Mike and asked him about his promise to stay sober. Mike promised to have only one beer and remain OK to drive.

At this, Scott thought to himself, "Is he really serious?" Throughout the evening, Scott watched as Mike took one cup and then another and another. Scott himself had three beers and would not even consider driving. Everyone else who came in the jeep was wasted. Scott did not know how many beers Mike had at the party, but he had the feeling that Mike was in no shape to drive. When it was time to head back to campus, Mike reassured Scott and the rest of the guys that he was fine.

As Scott stood ready to climb into the jeep, he could almost hear his own thought, "Should I be doing this?"

◼ Designated Driver

What is this case about?   Immerse yourself in this case by walking in Scott Duncan's shoes as he decides whether to get into the jeep for the ride back to campus after a fraternity party. He saw the designated driver drinking beer.

Get the facts.   List the facts that you know about Scott and his situation:

1. _____

2. _____

3. _____

4. _____

5. _____

State the problem, issue or question that needs to be resolved.

_____

_____

List several ways that the problem might be resolved.

1. _____

2. _____

3. _____

Write down the best way to solve the problem and why you would solve it that way.

_____

_____

_____

_____

Hopeless
Case Study

Hopeless

Her residence hall was quiet again this weekend and Caroline Whyte felt very lonely. Her roommate had a boyfriend with whom she spent most of her time and everyone else seemed to leave each weekend. Fall break was just around the corner and Caroline wanted to take that opportunity to go home and not come back.

■ Hopeless

Caroline Whyte looked out the window of her room and sighed heavily. It was quiet in her hall again this weekend, and she felt lonely. Her roommate was over at her boyfriend's place *again*. So far she was not happy at college and was thinking about calling it quits. "I don't like it here," she thought, "what's the point of staying?"

Hampton University was a long way from home. Caroline had expected it to be a little more familiar to her than it turned out to be. She had lived here once when she was five years old. Even though her family had lived in the Midwest for most of her life, Caroline wanted to come to school in the south for the university's sports administration program, and to "be different."

When she was registering for classes, Caroline's advisor recommended that she not take University 101, which was a course that helped freshmen students adjust to college. Almost all students at Hampton University take the class and everyone seems to think that it does help them. In the classes that she was taking, Caroline was doing pretty well. Her grades were mostly Bs so far. Caroline wondered if taking University 101 might have been a good idea.

Even though she was shy, Caroline got very involved in high school. College was a different story. She joined the sports administration club as soon as she was settled on campus; but she still did not feel like she was a part of things. Her roommate spent most of her time with her boyfriend. As she thought about it, she got more frustrated. "Why does everyone on my floor have to leave town every weekend?" It was hard to get to know people when they never seemed to be around. "It's not like my RA is ever here, either," she thought.

Caroline started calling her parents and her boyfriend every day and told them how much she disliked school. Her calls became so frequent that her mother called the hall director where Caroline lived to see if he might be able to help her get over her homesickness. There was a small light at the end of the tunnel: the four-day fall break was coming up and Caroline could not wait to go home. She wanted to go home and not come back, but her mother said that she should try to stick it out for the rest of the semester. Her dad wanted her to stay for the rest of the year, but the thought of that depressed her. Her dad thought that she just needed time to adjust. Caroline knew that she would hate it more each day.

Caroline did not want to be a disappointment to her parents, but she really wanted to leave school and not come back. She thought about what she could have done to make things better, but it seemed hopeless.

■ Hopeless

What is this case about?   Immerse yourself in this case by putting yourself in Caroline Whyte's shoes. Feel the loneliness of the weekend when her roommate was away visiting her boyfriend and everyone else had left campus for the weekend. Fall break is not far off and you just want to go home and not come back.

Get the facts.   List the facts that you know about Caroline and the situation:

1. _____

2. _____

3. _____

4. _____

5. _____

State the problem, issue or question that needs to be resolved.

_____

_____

List several ways that the problem might be resolved.

1. _____

2. _____

3. _____

Write down the best way to solve the problem and why you would solve it that way.

_____

_____

_____

_____

Let Go
Case Study

Let Go

Lynette DeMarco's mother called her two and sometimes three times a day to see if everything was okay. Her mother seemed to imagine the worst and her daily questioning frustrated Lynette. She wondered how she might convince her parents that she could take care of herself.

■ Let Go

Another phone call from Mom. "Where were you?" "What time did you get in?" "Who were you with?" Lynette hung up the phone after another uneasy conversation with her mother. "When will she just let go?" she wondered aloud in the quiet of her apartment.

Lynette DeMarco had been a freshman at the university only a few weeks, but things had settled down and she had developed a routine with which she was mostly comfortable. She lived about 10 minutes from campus in a one-bedroom apartment that she really liked because it was quiet and she could study without distractions. Its only drawback was that it made it difficult to meet people.

Lynette grew up in Cape May, New Jersey—the oldest resort town in the country. That was where her parents still lived after 25 years of marriage, and most of her relatives also lived close by. Her brother currently attended Slippery Rock University, but everyone else stayed pretty close to home. She never really understood why exactly, because her's was not a close family. She had even said to Laura, her best friend, "I'm uncomfortable around family, you can't talk with them like you can your friends. They're typical Northeasterners; never open with hugs and kisses."

Academic success was very important to Lynette. She studied diligently in high school and graduated valedictorian in a class of 250. Her SAT score was 1400 and with it she applied to some of the top colleges along the East coast, including Yale, Princeton, Boston University, Lafayette, University of Richmond, and University of South Carolina. With the exception of Princeton, she was accepted by all the colleges to which she applied. She chose the University of South Carolina because it was the farthest from home and had a highly respected international studies program.

Laura Heffler was Lynette's closest friend in high school. Their boyfriends were brothers, and the four of them hung out constantly together for the last two years, horseback riding and taking their mountain bikes for long day-trips into the hills around Cape May. Laura planned to move to South Carolina and share the apartment with Lynette while attending the community college there. But, a few weeks before the move, Laura was offered a modeling contract and a chance to audition on Broadway. She just could not turn it down, so she decided not to go to South Carolina.

Lynette's boyfriend had decided to attend the University of California at Santa Cruz. Because they would be separated by such a great distance, they decided that they could each date other people. That way they would learn for sure if they were meant to be with each other.

Moving to South Carolina was not as easy as Lynette had thought it would be. For the two weeks before she was to leave, her mother seemed to argue with her over everything. The arguments were over little things, but it was frustrating for Lynette. She heard lectures about locking doors and always having mace with her. Her parents were still upset about how Laura had left Lynette with the apartment lease. To Lynette, it seemed more time was spent reassuring everyone that she could take care of herself than was actually spent packing her things for the move.

Her parents and her grandmother drove her to South Carolina.

Emotions ran high when the time finally came for them to leave Lynette behind in her apartment and begin the return trip home. She could not believe it when she saw her mother, grandmother, and even her dad cry as they said good-bye. The scene was overwhelming. When the door shut and she found herself alone, she thought, "Wow, I'm here. Now, what do I do?"

She did not have long to wait. Her mom called her three times during the drive back to New Jersey. "Was she alright?" "Did she have everything she needed?"

For the next two weeks, Lynette's mom called her two or three times a day. Naturally, she was not always home when her mom called, and when that occurred she would later be drilled with questions; "Where were you? What time did you get in? Who were you with?" Her mother even called her at 8 a.m. on Saturday morning!

The calling and checking up on her frustrated Lynette. Her mother's habit of imagining the worst was unsettling. Today, as she hung up the phone, she wondered aloud, "What can I do to prove to my parents (and to myself) that I am going to be okay?"

■ Let Go

What is this case about?   Immerse yourself in this case by imagining that you are Lynette DeMarco and your mother calls two or three times a day. You want to convince your mother that you can take care of yourself.

Get the facts.   List the facts that you know about Lynette and her situation:

1. _____

2. _____

3. _____

4. _____

5. _____

State the problem, issue or question that needs to be resolved.

_____

_____

List several ways that the problem might be resolved.

1. _____

2. _____

3. _____

Write down the best way to solve the problem and why you would solve it that way.

_____

_____

_____

_____

The Chat Room
Case Study

The Chat Room

This case is about Bridget Spencer who, early in her freshman year at Midstate University, becomes hooked on the Internet and escapes into chat rooms where she "meets" a man and eventually gives him her phone number. The man begins to call to try to recruit her to perform in a porn movie. She is now afraid to answer the phone and fears that the man might come to campus looking for her.

◼ The Chat Room

Bridget Spencer was more addicted to the Internet than she thought she should be. As she sat locked in her dorm room, she knew that things had gone too far. "That guy in the chat room seemed nice enough," she thought, "how could I be so stupid to give him my number?"

Bridget did not have a computer of her own, but she wanted to learn how to use one. As a matter of fact, she had registered for University 101, Freshman Seminar, because in that course students learned how to use the Internet and got their own e-mail accounts. Her interest grew rapidly after her first three weeks in college.

During those weeks, Bridget was side-tracked by the party scene at Midstate University and her college career had gotten off to a rocky start. Too many parties led her to miss some of her classes and soon she found herself exhausted, disillusioned and disinterested. She wanted out and found an escape in computers. There she sought intellectual conversation and an opportunity to meet new and interesting people. One of her University 101 classmates, James Hillman, fueled her interest by introducing her to chat rooms on the Internet.

The chat rooms offered Bridget what she was looking for in her search for a new outlet at college; the opportunity to meet different people, to learn different cultures, to compare different ideas and to voice her own opinion. This was something the party scene could never offer her, "Because," as Bridget put it, "everyone else is too smashed to understand what you are saying."

This new world of chat rooms also offered Bridget relative anonymity which diminished her fear of being rejected because of how she looked. Her short, shiny black hair and long baggy pants and boots had brought taunts about her sexual orientation from some people in the past and had distracted them from getting to know the real Bridget. Equally important to her was the belief that chatting on the Internet was not half as hazardous as attending a party where somebody might put "roofies" in her drink and she would not remember what happened after that. "It was a way of keeping out of trouble," she liked to say.

For someone seeking relief from the boredom of television, parties and the opportunity to fill the time that her 12 credit hours of study did not fill, the chat room seemed the ideal environment in which to learn and have fun. It provided diversity (chatting to people of all ages, cultures and lifestyles), stimulation, stress relief and above all, a sense of security that she was out of harm's way, safe in the bowels of the university library. Three to four hours a day were spent in various chat rooms; "going off on somebody," "making someone else happy," "giving advice," and generally, "being cheered up." Once, she spent the whole night on the computer; when the library closed at midnight, she went to the engineering computer lab where she got on the computer until 9:00 am the next morning.

It was in one such chat room, "Hot Tub," that she first met "Percular," after using the handle, "Sheba, the Love Goddess" (she thought it fit her image in high school as a romantic, gypsy type). Percular seemed really nice and gave no indication that his intentions were anything but honorable, making only basic inquiries about her interests and hobbies, what she did at college and inquiring how her day had been. Bridget was aware that a lot of individuals on the 'Net indulged in "cyber sex," particularly those in the "Hot Tub," but he did not appear to be one of them. He told her that he was 25 years old, from Virginia, interested in rock concerts and reading and that he considered himself a romantic, all in all, she thought, "a pretty cool guy."

She explained it this way, "He never acted interested in cyber sex or anything, so I was thinking he was not a creep. About three weeks after I first communicated with him, and feeling comfortable about it, I sent him my telephone number. Then, he comes on the telephone . . ."

During the first telephone conversation, she remembered that he, "dilly dallied for a while, chatted about things in general and was very polite. Then he just said, 'Well, I'm in this network and we are very sexually oriented and we would like for you to think about joining our network and being a movie star.'" The movie, he explained, was to be about a lonely college girl who meets this guy in a bar and leaves with him, after which "stuff happens."

Then it clicked, "This is a porn movie and he is trying to recruit me!"

She mumbled something about him joking. He was perfectly serious she soon learned, and she abruptly ended the conversation.

He persisted with his calls. "They came at really inconvenient times," she recalled, "like seven in the morning or just when I was leaving for class." The number of calls increased and each time he pleaded with her to reconsider joining the network. Soon, Bridget was afraid to pick up the phone or to go out of her room, "just in case he came down," she remembered.

Blaming herself, Bridget wondered what this guy might do next. Frustrated and fearful, she wished her phone would never again ring and wondered what she might do to stop his harassing calls.

■ The Chat Room

What is this case about?   Immerse yourself in this case by placing yourself in Bridget Spencer's shoes. You have met a man on the Internet that is now calling you to perform in a porn movie. How can you deal with him?

Get the facts.   List the facts that you know about Bridget and the situation:

1. _____

2. _____

3. _____

4. _____

5. _____

State the problem, issue or question that needs to be resolved.

_____

_____

List several ways that the problem might be resolved.

1. _____

2. _____

3. _____

Write down the best way to solve the problem and why you would solve it that way.

_____

_____

_____

_____

The Eating Game
Case Study

The Eating Game

Emily LeBlanc had overcome her own eating disorder so she recognized the symptoms in Jeannie, one of her hall-mates. She wanted to say something to Jeannie, but knew that it would not be an easy thing to do.

■ The Eating Game

Emily had seen all the tricks, and had played most of them herself. She knew the signs of a eating disorder like frequently skipped meals, binge eating, and calorie counting. She had been a master of the eating game, and she suspected her hallmate, Jeannie, was playing it. But, this evening all her doubts were erased when she observed Jeannie's inability to find anything to eat at the dinner table. "Can I let Jeannie continue to play this game?" she whispered to herself.

Overweight

When Emily LeBlanc was 15-years-old and a sophomore in high school, she weighed 160 pounds and realized that she had to go on a diet if she were ever to wear cute outfits and be attractive to boys. Diet she did, and by the time she began her junior year she had lost 20 pounds. She was encouraged by her success and lost another 37 pounds during the first half of her junior year. Still, she saw herself as fat and was intensely afraid of gaining more weight. Her mother thought Emily had lost enough and was so concerned that she took her to a doctor during the winter break. It was then that Emily learned that she might have an eating disorder that caused her to lose weight far beyond what she should have for her height of 5'5". She began seeing a psychologist every week for the next year. During the last half of her senior year, her weight stabilized and she reduced her visits to the doctor to once a month.

The "Freshman Fifteen"

Emily entered South Central State University determined not to gain the "freshman 15," those new pounds that so many freshmen gain during their first few months away from home. She exercised rigorously and ate sparingly to lose 8 pounds after she arrived on campus. She quit seeing her psychologist since that involved driving home. Quite frankly, she enjoyed being away from home and away from her mother's constant questions about her eating. However, when her friends voiced concern about her weight, which had dropped to 108 pounds, she gained "five or maybe three pounds back."

Emily still worried about her weight, but she felt that she handled her eating disorder fairly well. She watched her diet carefully, making sure to get the proper proteins and vitamins. She was pleased that, even though she was not still seeing her doctor, she had not forced herself to throw up since she had been at the University. She had done that at home, but never let her mother know.

The Lunch Bunch

Jeannie lived on the same floor of the residence hall as Emily and shared a room with Sarah, one of Emily's friends. Although Emily and Jeannie were not good friends, they hung out with the same crowd and would often eat meals together with the same group of people. Emily noticed that Jeannie would always complain about being hungry, but would only eat a pretzel or yogurt for lunch. She also noted that Jeannie had started carrying around the special light butter that she herself used for her meals. When Jeannie spoke to her it was usually about exercising or the calories in different foods. Even Sarah expressed concern about Jeannie's eating habits.

Conflict

On this particular evening, Jeannie had just finished another skimpy salad insisting that she could not find anything to eat for dinner. She had eaten the same thing for lunch and Emily knew that there was plenty to eat for dinner including non-fattening foods like broiled chicken breasts and vegetables. In a few minutes the "lunch bunch" would walk back to their residence hall together, as they always did. Emily wondered if she should pull Jeannie aside and say something about her eating behaviors. Pulling her aside would be easy, talking about her eating would be a different story. Jeannie would likely get angry and deny any problems with her eating. As the group rose from their seats, Emily gazed toward the door and struggled with her thoughts. "Should I let her play this game?"

■ The Eating Game

What is this case about?   Put yourself in Emily's position and figure out how you would approach Jeannie whom you suspect has an eating disorder.

Get the facts.   List the facts that you know about Emily and the situation she finds herself in:

1. _____

2. _____

3. _____

4. _____

5. _____

State the problem, issue or question that needs to be resolved.

_____

_____

List several ways that the problem might be resolved.

1. _____

2. _____

3. _____

Write down the best way to solve the problem and why you would solve it that way.

_____

_____

_____

_____

The Lab Partner
Case Study

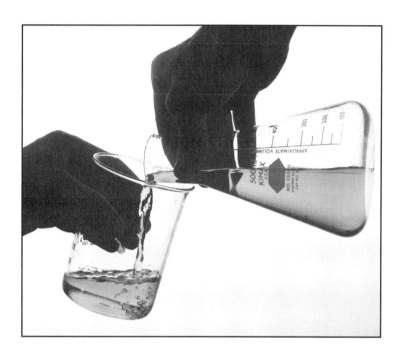

The Lab Partner

Pat Collins had to do all the work in lab. His lab partner just showed up assuming that his work would be done for him. Pat worried about what kind of grade he would get when he had to do everything himself.

■ The Lab Partner

Pat Collins reluctantly handed in his lab assignment to the teaching assistant. The lab today had been a complete disaster, and Pat worried that his grade would begin to be affected by the poor work that he and his lab partner were performing. But Pat had to do all of the work himself while his partner just showed up to class assuming that everything would be done for him. "I can't go on like this," Pat thought, "I'll never get a good grade if I am forced to do everything myself."

Pat was in the middle of his first semester at Mercury University. He came to MU from Maryland with a very good academic record, and decided to major in pharmacy after his experience working part-time in a drug store while in high school. He knew college would be challenging but did not know exactly how challenging it would be. Regardless, Pat was coming to school to study—not to party—so he was ready to accept the challenge.

During the first couple of weeks of the semester, Pat was without a lab partner for his chemistry class. A very conscientious student, he was worried that not having a lab partner would require additional work and would affect his grade. He had already called his mother to tell her that he had done poorly on a biology test, so he felt that he could not afford more work than would have been the case if he had a lab partner. But, Pat was very particular, so not having a partner allowed him to do the lab work exactly like he wanted it done. Two weeks into the course, Pat was finally assigned a partner and figured that things would begin to fall into place. But, instead of falling into place, things began to fall apart.

Pat's new lab partner was never prepared for class. He never read over the experiments or material before class and did not attend recitations. He did not study nor take any of the quizzes. He just came to the lab each week without any idea of how to perform the experiments. Unlike Pat, he was not in the least concerned about getting good grades. Pat wondered, "How can I possibly survive this semester in lab with this slacker?"

This week's experiment did not work the way it was supposed to and Pat blamed his lab partner's lack of preparation. Pat tried to save the experiment (without his partner's help), but it still did not come out right. That was not all; chemical problems and equations also had to be completed before the end of lab. Pat knew how to do the problems, but the failed experiment made doing the equations correctly much more difficult. As he worked through the problems he could feel the clock ticking away the time; he was running out of time.

Pat felt frustrated and angry. He was already in a bad mood when he arrived in lab, feeling tired and a little homesick. He missed his friends and family in Maryland. Making friends at Mercury was not as easy as he would like because he saw himself as somewhat more quiet and conservative than most others at the university. He did not really want to alienate his lab partner, and did his best not to be rude even though he was angry. He kept from confronting him because he was afraid that would make it too awkward to work with him in the future.

Pat turned in the assignment expecting a bad grade. The teaching assistant noticed the frustration and asked what was going on. Pat hesitated as he struggled for a way to respond.

■ The Lab Partner

What is this case about?   Get into the case by putting yourself in Pat Collins' place as he tries to figure out what to do about his lab partner who won't do any of the work.

Get the facts.   List the facts that you know about Pat and his situation:

1. _____

2. _____

3. _____

4. _____

5. _____

State the problem, issue or question that needs to be resolved.

_____

_____

List several ways that the problem might be resolved.

1. _____

2. _____

3. _____

Write down the best way to solve the problem and why you would solve it that way.

_____

_____

_____

_____

This Paper Is Plagiarized
Case Study

This Paper Is Plagiarized

This case depicts a freshman, Amy Sloan, being accused of plagiarism by her instructor. She is not sure how to respond. Her paper is included as an exhibit with this case.

■ This Paper Is Plagiarized

Amy Sloan could not believe what she was hearing. Her instructor, John Bell, had asked her to see him after class and now, as she stood in front of him near the classroom door, he handed her the paper she had turned in last week. She flipped the pages quickly and saw no marks, not even a grade. When she looked up, she heard him say, "This paper is plagiarized."

This was Amy's first semester as a college freshman and it had not been an easy start to college. Her family lived in a rather small town nearly an hour and a half distant. Her leaving home for the first time had not been easy for her mother. As a matter of fact, her mother had called several times in a state of near hysteria and Amy had responded by driving home to be with her and to help reassure her that everything was alright at college; she was still alive and healthy.

By going home, Amy had missed five class meetings of her freshman seminar course. She did not want her frequent absences to be a problem for her, so she had met with Mr. Bell and confided that she had a personal problem at home and had to be there on several days which had caused her to miss class. She showed him her journal, which was required for the course, and let him see that she had faithfully continued to write her journal entries even though she had not been in class. He seemed to understand.

The assignment required that students pick a topic and write a research paper using at least four sources of reference. Each student was also to give an oral report to the class on the research paper they had done. Amy decided to write about schizophrenia since she had done a lot of reading about that subject and knew quite a bit about it.

This was Amy's first college paper, so she did not know exactly what to expect. She liked to write and had been encouraged by her high school teachers who often told her that she was a good writer. That encouragement had led her to experiment with her writing and she had done some poetry and short stories. She felt comfortable and successful with her writing and had chosen English as her major.

And now she listened in shock as Mr. Bell continued, "It's not a regular research paper, you couldn't have written it. No freshman could write this kind of paper!"

She looked back down at her paper (Exhibit 1), and, with a rising sense of panic, she searched for the right words with which to explain.

EXHIBIT 1

Schizophrenia: an overview of the disease
and one woman's struggle for sanity.
September 19, 1995

Lori Shiller was the perfect child in what seemed like the perfect family. She had loving parents and two brothers that looked up to her. She was a straight "A" student, was very involved with high school, and had a very bright future in front of her. The suburb she and her family lived in had an extremely high status and was very wealthy. At seventeen she was working as a camp counselor at Lincoln Farm Summer Camp. and it was there that she heard them for the first time. she heard something that no one else heard at the time and that no one would ever hear. "You must die! You must die! You will die!"

Not knowing what was wrong with her, she tried her hardest to keep it inside. but the rest of the camp staff started to notice a change in her always perky attitude. They noticed how spaced out she was and that she was extremely depressed. She was sent home. Her parents were on vacation at the time, so there would be no questions asked and she would have a few days to get herself together. She hid the screaming voices inside her head and went on with life as normal.

The next fall she began her college career at Tufts University. She shared an apartment with two of her closest friends. She tried to conceal the voices even though they became more frequent and sinister. Her mood changes became violent and threatened the lives of her roommates and herself. At twenty-three she made her first suicide attempt. The was the first warning of a secret disease taking root in her mind.

Her parents were shocked at the thought of Lori being mentally ill, and kept thinking that she was just depressed and that everything would work itself out. The staff at the Payne Whitney Clinic in New York had different ideas. Lori was breaking down. Almost every person she came into contact with was showered with the voices in Lori's mind. They shouted at her, threatened her, and gave her ideas of killing everyone. The voices not only talked to her and wouldn't let her sleep at night, they occupied her every moment. Then the hallucinations began. At some moments she would look at her hands and they would be splitting open oozing blood. This type of occurrence became a normality.

Even after the doctors diagnosed Lori with chronic Schizophrenia, she still thought nothing of her illness. She found the voices irritating, but had no idea of its seriousness. Lore couldn't believe that no one heard the voices she heard. She was self conscious around others because of it. She was discharged from the hospital with the idea that she would live at home under supervision. Lori convinced the doctors that she could do it on her own. This was her parents and her doctors first mistake.

On her own, Lori attended day classes at the hospital while her parents worked. But soon she found it easy to skip the classes and began hanging out with the wrong people. She started doing cocaine because it helped smother the voices, but her habit turned into something she could not handle. Her parents began to threaten her about ending her drug habit and she had a mental relapse. She tried to commit suicide again and was forcibly hospitalized.

Lori had gained almost fifty pounds by this point, weighing in at one hundred and seventy pounds which was far from her normal, slim physique. A lot of the weight gain came from heavy medication, but depression played a key role as well. Lori had been pulled into the mental health care system and eventually was hospitalized five different times. She had many relapses, two suicide attempts, and a screaming, full-blown schizophrenia that seemed beyond the reach of any cure.

Two women, and incredible staff, a loving family, a self-examination, and a newfound will to live pulled Lori out of madness and she began to cope. Lori co-wrote her book The Quiet Room, she has a job on weekends, and devotes a lot of her time to mental patients and their families. But there one thing in her past that will be with her forever . . . The voices. (Bennett, Shiller, The Quiet Room)

Schizophrenia in a literal sense means "split mind", but the disease does not imply a split personality. It is not someone acting like two different people. Schizophrenia was not distinguished from other forms of psychosis until the twentieth century. (Achernect, 92)

Schizophrenia almost always develops before middle age. The first episode normally takes place sometime during adolescence or young adulthood and is followed by other increasingly detrimental episodes. The disease causes deterioration in a person's work, social relationships, and ability to look after himself or herself. (Wolman, 195)

The symptoms of schizophrenia are not routine and are not the same for every individual. Some common symptoms include isolation from family and friends, hallucinations, perpetual problems, sudden disturbances in movement, and odd speech and behavior. (Wolman, 198) "Being unable to control one's own thoughts, being isolated by a vision of reality all one' own, being commanded to act by disembodied voices-these are the experiences that make schizophrenia such a frightening experience." (Shiller, 278)

Scientists agree that schizophrenia has not single cause. It is the product of an interplay of biology, psychology, and culture. The disease does tend to be genetically inherited. It is more likely to affect someone that is a close relative to a schizophrenic than the population at large. Whereas only one or two out of every one-hundred people become schizophrenic over a life time, about ten out of every one hundred children who have one schizophrenic parent eventually will develop the disorder. (Wender, 115)

Whether schizophrenia is caused by a biochemical abnormality, a neurological defect, or a bad enzyme is still open to question. Most scientists believe that the strength and severeness of the disease varies from one individual to another. (Brunner, 177)

Research has led to some breakthroughs linking a number of environmental factors to schizophrenia. For example, unclear communication within families is one potential condition, although scientists are still unsure whether miscommunication in the family is a cause of schizophrenia or an after effect. Poverty has also been associated with the disease. (Brunner, 181)

The most powerful treatment for alleviating schizophrenic symptoms is antipsychotic medication. (Horwitz, 54) These drugs have for the first time enabled patients to function without breakdowns or unpleasant symptoms. They are used to hault episodes of schizophrenia and also to prevent future problems. These drugs, however, do have drawbacks. They can produce minor side effects such as drowsiness and dry mouth and can also have long term consequences. Some patients that use the drugs for a long period of time develop a condition known as tardive dyskinesia. This disease is characterized by abnormal movements of the mouth and tongue. This is especially serious because tardive dyskinesia has no known cure and may not disappear once the patient stops using the drug. Not every patient benefits from antipsychotic drugs, and some seem not to need them at all. Some forms of psychotherapy are also used to treat schizophrenic patients. It is also used to help patients who do not receive medication. (Maisto, 97-9)

Schizophrenia is a dangerous disease that often times causes its victims to totally withdraw from society and from their normal routines. Even though in the past it was thought as only as "abnormal." or "weird", the disease known as schizophrenia is now taken seriously, and continual breakthroughs are being made to help it's victim. The disease still has not cure-only ways to lesson the symptoms and the voices. "The voices taught me about a hell that was beyond all religious beliefs, It was beyond all imagining, beyond all human hope. The voices that spoke to me were as clear and as real as any voices around me. In fact, they were more real, because they were both inside me and outside me.

"Come to me," they crooned. "Come to hell with me."

I didn't want to listen. I didn't want to hear. But I had no choice. Where would I go?" L. Shiller

Bibliography

Ackernecht, E. H. *A Short History of Psychiatry*. Hafner, 2d ed., rev., 1970.

A Casebook in Psychiatric Ethics. Brunner/Mazell, 1990.

Bennett, Amanda and Shiller, Lori. *The Quiet Room*: A Journey Out of the Torment of Madness.

Horwitz, Elinor Lander. *Madness, Magic, and Medicine*: the Treatment and Mistreatment of the Mentally Ill. Lippincott, 1977.

Maisto, Stephen A. and others. *Drug Use and Misuse*. Holt, Rinehart, and Winston, 1991.

Wender, Paul H. and Klein, Donald F. *Mind, Mood, and Medicine*: A guide to the New Biopsychiatry. Farrar, 1981.

Wolman, Benjamin B., ed. *International Encyclopedia of Psychiatry, Psychoanalysis, and Neurology*. 12v. Van Nostrand, 1977.

◼ This Paper Is Plagiarized

What is this case about?   Immerse yourself in this case by reading the paper that Amy Sloan turned in only to have her instructor say it was plagiarized. If this was your paper, how would you respond?

Get the facts.   List the facts that you know about Amy and her situation:

1. _____

2. _____

3. _____

4. _____

5. _____

State the problem, issue or question that needs to be resolved.

_____

_____

List several ways that the problem might be resolved.

1. _____

2. _____

3. _____

Write down the best way to solve the problem and why you would solve it that way.

_____

_____

_____

_____

Wish You Were Here
Case Study

■ Wish You Were Here

A young freshman, Ruth Swenson, was happy at college and adjusted very well to her new surroundings. Her mother, however, had not adjusted to having her daughter away and called often asking her to come home for a weekend visit. Feeling guilty, Ruth went home for a weekend in October, but by Saturday afternoon was ready to return to college.

■ Wish You Were Here

Ruth Swenson had given in. She had finally gone home to visit. Everything looked about the same. The street had new paving and her dad had done a little redecorating, but nothing much had changed. She could not help but think about how much she would love to get back to school. She had only been home for one day, but she wanted to say good-bye and get back to life at college.

Ruth was a freshman in her first semester at Clickman College. She had developed a great circle of friends and was pleased with her grades and progress in school so far. Unfortunately, she could not help but feel guilty about not spending time at home in Anderson, a small town about an hour and a half away from the college. She loved her mother, at times she even considered her mom to be her very best friend. But, Ruth had grown tired of having the same conversation with her every time she called, which had become about three times a week.

"Ruth, why don't you ever come home for a visit? You dad works every night anymore and you know how your brother is. . . . I really miss not having you around. Why don't you come home, we're only an hour and a half away?"

Ruth always gave the same reply, "Mom . . . Mom . . . stop making me feel so guilty! I'd love to come home but I'm *really* busy this week. I have a paper due on Tuesday and I have plans to go to the game with some friends from my hall on Saturday. Besides, I'll be home for Thanksgiving next month."

"Oh . . . I know. I understand," she sighed. "I went away to college and left my folks at home way back when. It's alright."

"Okay then. So what else is new . . ."

"But," her mom interrupted, "I get so lonely and I was just thinking about how nice it would be to have you come home for a visit."

These conversations always made Ruth feel so guilty. Why did her mom always have to say, "I miss you" and "I'm lonely?" Every time Ruth was having fun or was about to go out on a Friday night with her friends, she couldn't help but think of her mom sitting at home all alone wishing her only daughter would come home to visit. She thought to herself, "Why can't Mom realize that I have a life here at Clickman?"

Her brother, Eric, was also away at college but too busy to visit with Mom. Plus, he did not have the same relationship with their mother that Ruth had. She knew her father was around sometimes, but he worked a lot and Ruth did not have much to say to him anyway. She knew he loved her, and that was enough.

On the third weekend in October, Ruth finally gave in and drove home Friday afternoon intending to stay until Sunday. On Saturday afternoon she realized how much she really wanted to be at Clickman. "How can I say good-bye," she wondered.

■ Wish You Were Here

What is this case about?   Put yourself in Ruth Swenson's shoes. Your mother misses you and wants you to come home and visit. You do, but after a day you're ready to return to college.

Get the facts.   List the facts that you know about Ruth and her situation:

1. _____

2. _____

3. _____

4. _____

5. _____

State the problem, issue or question that needs to be resolved.

_____

_____

List several ways that the problem might be resolved.

1. _____

2. _____

3. _____

Write down the best way to solve the problem and why you would solve it that way.

_____

_____

_____

_____

Wounded Freshman
Case Study

◼ Wounded Freshman

In this case, Ann Williamson is angry and embarrassed when her English instructor criticizes her paper in front of the class.

Ann Williamson wanted to run out of class and go as far away as her legs would carry her. She had just been "called out" by her English instructor in front of the whole class and was boiling with anger and embarrassment. "Is this the way they treat freshmen?" she wondered as she tried to control the hurt she felt.

Ann was one of 20 freshmen in English 101, English Composition. It was a special class for the limited number of students who had been admitted to the university on probation. Each of these students were required to complete a prescribed curriculum of 30 semester hours with a C grade average during their freshman year in order to continue their studies at the university. It was a "all or nothing" chance to prove themselves. Ann felt the pressure. She had never enjoyed school and always found it difficult. High academic achievement was not one of her strengths and she knew that she would have to work hard and focus a lot of attention on her grades.

It was the end of September, about a month past the last day to add or drop classes, Dr. Elizabeth Olsen, her English professor and academic adviser, had assigned the class to write a personal reflection paper about a lesson they had learned at some point in their lives. Ann was unsure about what to write. As usual, she felt that Dr. Olsen's instructions were unclear. She always seemed to make vague assignments and was unwilling to elaborate when asked for clarification. The students had quit asking. Instead, they just guessed at what they thought she might want. They had learned that she would somehow make them look stupid if they asked. In a condescending tone she would say, "Sweetheart" (she never used a student's name), "you'll never get out of here if you can't understand simple instructions. No one's going to hold your hand. You just have to figure some things out on your own."

Everyone in class tried to "lay low" and keep from being noticed. But, Dr. Olsen required that students bring their first draft to class and she would quickly read and comment on it. That could be a mortifying experience. Ann heard her tell a classmate, "Honey, this is not what I'm looking for. You need to start over from scratch."

Ann felt herself begin to panic. She was not comfortable with the paper she had written and did not want Dr. Olsen to read it just yet. Dr. Olsen must have seen her expression and began moving in her direction. Ann, usually very quiet in class, blurted out, "I'm not sure this is what you wanted."

Dr. Olsen picked up Ann's paper and began scanning it. "The caliber of this work is pretty low. Actually, it's just trash," she commented loudly.

Upset and embarrassed, Ann looked down at her desk with a desperate thought, "Please no, not in front of the class."

◼ Wounded Freshman

What is this case about?   Immerse yourself in this case by putting yourself in Ann
Williamson's place. She has just been criticized by her instructor
in front of the class.

Get the facts.   List the facts that you know about Ann and her situation:

1. _____

2. _____

3. _____

4. _____

5. _____

State the problem, issue or question that needs to be resolved.

_____

_____

List several ways that the problem might be resolved.

1. _____

2. _____

3. _____

Write down the best way to solve the problem and why you would solve it that way.

_____

_____

_____

_____